ry of Congress Catalog Card Number: 83-62164

N: 0-688-02515-3

ted in the United States of America

Edition

3 4 5 6 7 8 9 10

Jack Kent Cooke who conceived;
bby Beathard who believed; and
e Gibbs who achieved.
nally, to John Riggins and Joe Theismann
ho waited so long, and both worked so
edicatedly during the wonderful season of
982, for a Super Bowl ring. And especially
Vince and Juanita McMahon.

The author specifically wants to express his gratitude to
a number of people who aided with the compilation of
material for this book under an extremely tight deadline,
namely: Charley Taylor of the Washington Redskins; Nat
Fine of the Washington Redskins; Fran Connors of the
American Football Conference; Dick Maxwell of the National Football Conference; Mickey Palmer for some of
the color photography and two artists in their own right,
Gerry Repp who designed the book and Barbara Hov-
sepian who eliminated the dangling participles.

THE REDSKI

BY LOU SAHADI

1 2

To
B
J
Fi
w
d
1
t

WILLIAM MORROW AND COMPANY, INC.
New York   1983

CONTENTS

FAN MANIA 1
"It Was Something I Never Experienced Before"

HAIL TO THE REDSKINS
Hail to the Redskins
  Hail Victory
Braves on the warpath
  Fight for old D.C.

Run or pass and score—
  We want a lot more
Beat 'em Swamp 'em Touchdown—
  Let the points soar
Fight on, Fight on—
  Till you have won
Sons of Wash-ing-ton.

The fight song has been heard around the National Football League ever since 1937. Back then, Franklin Delano Roosevelt was serving his second term as President, and Washington had a major league baseball team called the Senators. All that is left now are the Washington Redskins and their endearing fans who have used the football team as a rallying ground. There isn't another team in professional football with a collegiate fight song that is heard before every game and after each victory, and there isn't another one either that has sold out 122 consecutive home games over the years. They are there every Sunday, loud and colorful, some in Indian headdress, others with painted faces, others wielding signs. They all have a genuine love for the Redskins. Their behavior at times borders on maniacal. It hasn't gone unnoticed by Washington coach Joe Gibbs who believes the Redskins' fans are worth a touchdown each game. In a sense, the Redskin fan is a phenomenon.

This was never more apparent than after the glorious Redskins defeated the Miami Dolphins in Super Bowl XVII some 3,000 miles away from Washington. Barely 72 hours later, the city hailed its heroes with an official victory parade. President Reagan allowed government employees two hours off from their jobs to view it. By the same token, students were allowed to miss school, even though two years before, they weren't given permission to witness President Reagan's inauguration. They were all part of a crowd of 500,000 that lined Constitution Avenue to cheer the Redskins.

The magnitude of the crowd astounded the parade officials. Because of the day-long rain that had begun that morning, they expected perhaps half that

Coach Joe Gibbs, smiling left, reacts to the reading of a proclamation honoring the Redskins by Virginia Governor Chuck Robb, right, following Super Bowl victory parade in Washington that attracted half-million fans despite day-long rain. Center is Fred Herzog, master of ceremonies.

number. Maybe the rain was an omen. It was looked on as "Hog Weather," and what better setting to come out and cheer for a wonderful bunch of hogs who had created such a tumultuous season. The crowd was so big the officials had to abandon the idea of having each player ride in a convertible. Instead, as a safeguard, the players remained in the two busses that had brought them from their training compound across the Potomac River into such unexpected celebration.

"There's nowhere for the parade to go," said a veteran police officer on the scene. "They've got both sides of the route jammed wall to wall with people. You can't get a scooter through there, let alone a parade."

After a delay created by the surging crowd, the parade did take place through a mass of humanity almost a mile long. Many of the fans were gripped with hysteria, jumping up and down, breaking through the police lines to pound on the sides of the slow-moving busses.

"It was something I never experienced before," the injured wide receiver Art Monk said afterwards. "It makes you feel that you accomplished something and that the whole community is behind you. It sends a chill through your body."

What accounts for such emotionalism on the part of Redskin fans? The intense loyalty they project is predicated on the fact that the Redskins are the only establishment all Washingtonians share in common. The city is held together by geography and politics. Its work force lives in three different political jurisdictions: Virginia, Maryland and the District of Columbia. The Redskins are the rallying cry for one and all, Republicans and Democrats alike.

Most Washington area residents come from other states. Thus a large share of them still maintain a rooting interest for their hometown teams. However, much of this has changed with the success of the Redskins. For example, it brought about a switch in loyalties in Richard Rodin, who was born on Long Island, played basketball at Columbia and was a devout New York Giants fan. An attorney, Rodin is one of several thousand fortunate Redskin season ticket holders.

"Like a lot of people," Rodin explained, "I came here to work for the Government and took things year by year. But when I left the Government and joined a law firm, it was a decision to stay here and become a Washingtonian. That's when it happened. I became a Redskin fan."

Former United States Senator Eugene McCarthy from Minnesota draws a deeper parallel, namely that football and politics have much in common. Since Washington is the largest political city in the nation, it is only natural that football and politics should be drawn together. The basis of his belief was formed at the first Touchdown Club dinner he ever attended.

"The closeness of football to politics was underscored by the speeches given by the recipients of the awards," McCarthy recalled. "Through the whole range of award winners, from the pros to grade school players, the speeches were almost identical, not only with one another but also with the speeches I've heard through the years at victory parties following successful elections. Football players and politicians alike run through the list of persons—the same list—to whom they owe their success. The titles in some cases are slightly different, but the function and the contribution are the same.

"Fathers and mothers are thanked, teammates, or campaign workers, the coach or campaign director, wives in some cases, and also understanding children, particularly among the pros; student bodies and the fans or one's constituents in the case of politicians. And these are followed by promises of dedicated service and future victories.

"A further identification between the game of football and politics is manifest in the transferability of figures of speech, of metaphor. This transfer was especially noticeable during the Administration of Richard Nixon, when the President demonstrated a greater interest in football than had any of his immediate predecessors. To the great chagrin of Joe Paterno, in 1969 he even went so far as to pick Texas as the No. 1 team over Penn State.

"Subordinates in that Administration, evidently aware of the President's interest in the game, began to use football language either to get to him or to explain his policies. Thus his Secretary of Defense described the bombings of North Vietnam as 'Operation Linebacker,' and when he was under some pressure to explain why the Vietnamese army was not performing very well, he urged critics to be patient and remember that they were an expansion team.

"Mixing politics and football images, critics of the Eisenhower Administration said the Administration's best offensive play and best groundgainer was the 'forward fumble.' And of the Carter Administration, the problem was that it 'always punted on first down.'"

Obviously, the chemistry of football and politics mixes well in Washington. At a reception honoring the Super Bowl champions, Washington mayor Marion Berry said that the Redskins had helped to bring Washingtonians together. Senator Paula Hawkins, Republican from Florida, wore a Redskin jersey to the affair even though she was rooting for the Dolphins in the game. And Representative Michael Barnes, Democrat of Maryland, felt the Redskins' success helped him overcome some bad childhood memories. "I remember rooting in Griffith Stadium for the old Washington Deadskins," said Barnes.

By the time Governor Charles Robb arrived at the reception, he was drenched from the rain. It didn't bother him. "My clothes got wet, and I'll probably catch a cold, but it was worth it," said Robb.

Just like it was worth it to Sam Legard to travel 3,000 miles to California to cook ribs for the Redskin players. During the season it had been a ritual he performed one evening a week after practice. The players felt that Legard cooked some "mean" ribs. Yet, the Super Bowl was a new challenge to him. Much to the delight of the players, he somehow arranged to have his two big barbecues transported to the coast by plane.

It was only fitting that Legard got to do this thing out west. That's where the business of barbecuing originated. A few short days later, the Redskin players made sure that Legard's long journey wasn't wasted. ●

JACK KENT COOKE 2
"This Is My Third Life"

When owner Jack Kent Cooke decided to leave the West Coast and move to Washington in the spring of 1979, he found a Redskin team mired in transition. George Allen had left; and general manager Bobby Beathard and coach Jack Pardee, under the direction of club president Edward Bennett Williams, were trying to rebuild the Redskins. In Pardee's first year as coach in 1978, Washington could manage only a .500 season after just having missed the playoffs in Allen's last season in 1977 with a 9-5 record.

The situation was not an unusual one for Cooke who had achieved success not only in business but with several other sport franchises. Prior to coming to Washington, he had owned The Forum in Los Angeles where his two other sport teams, the Los Angeles Lakers and the Los Angeles Kings, played. Cooke's teams were successful. The Lakers had appeared in the playoffs so many times and had won an NBA championship while the Kings, an expansion team in the NHL, had a better than average record. In March of 1979 Cooke sold The Forum, Lakers, and Kings and headed east.

During the years that Cooke lived on the West Coast, he had frequent contact with Williams, who kept him informed as to what was transpiring with the Redskins. Williams' pride in those years was the geriatric Allen and his "Over The Hill Gang." At 66, Cooke was determined to take an active role in the future success of the Redskins. There was more than one Washington observer, however, who wondered what drastic changes would take place with the arrival of Cooke. Primarily, how much of Bennett's powers would be usurped. Cooke had always been his own man, but Bennett had always been the management image reflected by the Redskins.

"The answer is very simple," Cooke said. "Not a jot. Ed Bennett Williams is still the presiding man. We've had telephonic dialogue for years. Regularly."

For the time being, nothing had to be done. During Cooke's first autumn in Washington, the Redskins played very well. After two months of the season, they produced a 6-2 record which was creditable enough to make any owner think about the winter playoffs. Cooke himself was not amazed by the performance even though the team had won only eight games the entire 1978 season.

"Surprised? Not particularly because I have such confidence in Bobby Beathard," Cooke said. "During a very pleasant, informal meeting I had with Bobby sometime in August, he predicted very much what the Redskins have done already. We don't know what the future holds, but I imagine the future will be bright. I have such confidence in Bobby and Jack Pardee that I don't worry too much. I would have been disappointed had Bobby and Jack not proceeded according to the predictions made, which is the other side of the coin, isn't it?

"But I'm pleased, and Ed Bennett Williams shares the same pinnacle of pleasure with the performance of the team to date. And just think, it's going to get better and better as the years go by. Take a look at their ages. Pardee and Beathard have been successful to date; I can't imagine them not continuing their winning ways. I like what they've done, and I think most all observers do. More kudos than ever to Bobby and Jack and the coaches and the players. The players, they are the ones who have to perform; and they are doing just that. They are doing it."

With Cooke closely observing that first year, the Redskins finished 10-6 and just missed getting into the playoffs. In 1980, the Redskins' bright future, which Cooke had anticipated, suddenly paled. The team suffered its first losing season in a decade, finishing with a 6-10 record. Cooke faced his first major crisis since assuming the operations of the Redskins. Beathard insisted that Pardee be dismissed. He based his reasoning on the fact that Pardee was depending more on older players who were going downhill instead of giving the younger ones an opportunity to build for the future. Beathard risked his job in recommending the coaching change. After conferring with Pardee, Cooke agreed with Beathard's analysis, fired Pardee, and placed the hiring of a new coach strictly in Beathard's hands. Whoever would replace Pardee, the "1979 Coach of the Year," most assuredly had to be better or the media would come down hard on management.

Yet, adversity was no stranger to Cooke. "This is my third life," Cooke said. "My first was in Canada, the second in California, and now here. I might as well start over."

His "first life" in Canada was something out of a Horatio Alger scenario. He was born in Toronto in 1912. The Great Depression all but eliminated the family wealth. At 21, he was married, broke, and faced an unstimulating career selling encyclopedias door to door. He was on his honeymoon, of all things, selling encyclopedias when his 1930 Ford Roadster became stuck in two feet of mud. Cooke remembers it as if it were yesterday and recalls this experience with the exuberance of someone 50 years younger.

"Veregin, Saskatchewan," Cooke began. "Veregin. Named after Veregin, who was the leader of the Diukabhoors. They were a strange sect in western Canada who used to parade in the nude, whenever in hell they didn't like what the local government was doing. So help me, God.

"I went out and saw the local grain elevator operator and the local minister and the local doctor, whatever the hell I could stop. Until, finally, school was out, and I saw the local principal. He didn't want to buy a set of books. I was with him from about 4:30 to 7:00 pm. His wife had dinner on the table. She kept giving me dirty looks as much as to say, 'Get out of here.'

"I was hungry. I knew my wife was hungry. By now she had walked from the car and was sitting in the kitchen of the hotel. And I think more to get rid of me than anything else, the principal gave me a $5 deposit on a set of books. The New Educator Encyclopedia. A perfectly dreadful set of encyclopedia. I got the car out of the mud, we bought a sandwich or two, and from then on my luck, in terms of post-dated checks, began to turn."

Perhaps nobody in Canada sold more encyclopedias than the determined Cooke. He sold so many he became a district manager for the company. He wasn't satisfied, and after a short while started his own company, which he didn't have long before Colgate-Palmolive hired him in an executive sales position. However, Cooke had higher goals. He decided to invest in a newspaper; he invested in others. Then he turned to radio and television investments. By the time he was 30 years old, Cooke was a self-made millionaire. He moved into other areas, purchasing plastic companies and tool and die firms. Cooke even tried to bring major league baseball to Toronto in 1959 when Branch Rickey announced the formation of the Continental League.

After his short-lived retirement in California, Cooke began operating again as if he had never left the business world. He started TelePrompter Corporation and became involved in other business ventures. One of his moves was to purchase the famous Chrysler Building in New York. Life was a joy again to Cooke. A suave dresser and eloquent speaker, he is perhaps the most charming owner among the 27 other NFL lodge brothers.

Cooke appeared happy in his active role with his team. He found a country estate in the rolling hills of Virginia near Upperville, some 50 miles from RFK Stadium where he became a regular visitor on Sundays. He shed his image of a California millionaire with a 16,000-acre ranch and

Joe Gibbs hands owner Jack Kent Cooke the game ball following Super Bowl XVII as running back John Riggins looks on.

became a country gentleman with a desire to influence a new era of Redskin history. Cooke was now a visible part of the Redskins, not only appearing at every game, but at practice sessions, as well.

"I love life here in northern Virginia," Cooke disclosed. "These are solid people, really solid people in this neck of the woods. Rather conservative, and I like that. Cautious, prudent, highly sensible people. They're earthy people, and this is beautiful country."

Cooke believed in his team even if others did not.

In 1981, the Redskins had a new coach. In fact, so new that Redskin fans had never before heard of Joe Gibbs, the offensive coordinator of the San Diego Chargers. The first five weeks of the season were unpleasant for Cooke. The team dropped five straight games, and Cooke began to hear whispers of the monumental mistake he had made in approving Gibbs as coach. His Sunday morning journeys to the stadium were lonely.

"Going to the stadium was all right," Cooke said, "because I went early when there wasn't anybody there except the fellow selling programs, and he'd say hello. But then, if I judge it correctly, even that fellow began looking at me with a jaundiced eye. It was coming out after we'd lose that was a hardship. The things people called me. Not your ordinary curse words. They were words of the vilest stripe. Really. What was I to do? I simply put my head down and went to my car."

Cooke derived some measure of satisfaction once the season ended. Washington won eight of its remaining eleven games to finish 8-8. His conviction to stay with Beathard, and ultimately, Gibbs, was substantially stronger now. He waited for the 1982 season with a great deal of hope and promise. While Cooke professed a belief in the Redskins, there were many who did not. The strike-shortened season didn't dispel Cooke's hopes either, because he felt deeply that the Redskins were on the way to playoff contention. All season long he maintained that position, and the Redskins didn't disappoint him. They finished with the best record in the NFL and a triumphant ending in the Super Bowl. In a moment of déjà vu, Cooke arrived for the game in Los Angeles, the same city where he had enjoyed his great sports success with the Lakers.

"I would not call this a triumphant return," Cooke said shortly after his arrival. "I'm making it with a certain amount of pleasure and happiness. How shall I put it? I have never enjoyed the hobby of owning a sports team as much as I am enjoying these Redskins. In baseball, soccer, hockey and basketball, my teams have won many championships. But, truly, this team transcends all of them for satisfaction and enjoyment.

"Is it possible—I don't know—that the San Francisco 49ers and Bill Walsh caught lightning in a bottle last year? Joe Gibbs and his incomparable coaching staff didn't have to catch lightning in a bottle. They're building a house on solid ground, whereas some teams may have built on sand, saying, 'To hell with tomorrow.' It's possible we're building for a good future. For example, we are accused of having no stars. We have stars. Many of our players are all-pro material. It's just that they are not yet recognized as such.

"This team is arriving, and I am glad it hasn't arrived fully yet, because when something arrives, it begins to leave. As long as we play as a coordinated, cohesive whole, we can compete with anybody. Not only compete, but in this season at least, win 90 percent of our games. The Redskins are unique inasmuch as we operate much like hard-working, intelligent in-company executives—with the board of directors being the assistant coaches, the executive vice president being Bobby Beathard, the president being Joe Gibbs and the chairman of the board being me. Most teams—most—in professional sports do not operate that way.

"Keeping Bobby was a great move, the most important thing I've done. Call it instinct, call it intuition, but the more I saw how well prepared Joe Gibbs was, how he knew what he wanted to do with the Redskins, I knew this was the man for the Redskins and for me—and boy, did he ever prove it."

Somehow, it all seemed to fall into place when Cooke himself assumed an active role with the Redskins a few years ago. He may never retire again.... ●

In 1979, Cooke moved from the West Coast and assumed an active role with the Redskins.

BOBBY BEATHARD

"When I Came Here In 1978 A Lot Of People Thought I Was Crazy"

In the cauldron of Washington politics, Bobby Beathard is unique. He is refreshingly low key and doesn't mind telling anyone that the only course he failed in college was political science. That alone would be sufficient to keep his name off the guest list of the "in" crowd at the many cocktail parties that are synonymous with the Washington scene. On the contrary, Beathard is probably one of the most popular figures in Washington, in or out of government. His stimulating candor arouses the stodgy atmosphere of any social gathering, which is why he receives so many invitations. Politely, Beathard refuses to attend, simply because he doesn't like to wear a shirt and tie. His disdain for wearing a suit isn't just affect; he genuinely abhors it. Beathard is more comfortable wearing jeans and sneakers which he does every day working as general manager for the Washington Redskins.

Since he admittedly cannot use a computer and doesn't really have a head for business, he is also unusual among his peers in the business atmosphere that professional football has become. He prefers the outdoors, and if he had remained in California where he grew up, or in Miami where he gained his knowledge of the game, he would probably have been more comfortable. All this is fine, except general managers in the National Football League's kingdom aren't supposed to be like that. Yet, perhaps it was Beathard's indifference to these standards that set him apart from the others who said he was crazy to accept the job club president Edward Bennett Williams offered him in 1978.

The talent erosion from the George Allen era was frightening. In manifesting his "future is now" theory, Allen generously traded away the club's draft choices for veterans. Unequivocally, the "Over The Hill Gang" captured Washington's fancy and generated so much national attention that even President Nixon proclaimed his support for the Redskins. Before he took the unenviable task of rebuilding the Redskins, Beathard knew the danger that existed because Allen had mortgaged the team's future somewhere near the national debt. Perhaps it was his special personality that made Beathard give Williams his honest opinion. In Washington, that was an admirable trait, and Williams was pleased.

"When I came here in 1978 a lot of people thought I was crazy," Beathard smiled. "I told Williams that we were in real trouble, that you've got a lot of old players, and you don't have any young players to take their place. You don't have any quickness, speed or strength."

Williams, a prominent attorney, must have been taken aback by Beathard's veracity. He accepted the fact that the Redskins were indeed in trouble and let Beathard take the club in a new direction. At first, Beathard didn't have anywhere to go. He believed that successful teams in pro football were created through the draft, which in Washington was a foreign area.

"It was frustrating when I first came in," Beathard recalled. "We just didn't have any draft choices left. We didn't have anything to work with, and yet we had all these scouts who wanted to work and do a good job. I was excited about the opportunity, but not the draft situation. We didn't have a draft pick until the sixth round. We sat there the whole first day of the draft. It was kind of frustrating, but to the scouts who'd been with the Redskins all along, it was no big deal. They were used to it. I got so excited when the sixth round came and the player we liked, running back Tony Green of Florida, was still there."

The Redskin fans were not too happy with Beathard's first move before the draft. It reminded them of George Allen's trade policies. Beathard traded Washington's number one draft choice to Cincinnati for cornerback Lemar Parris and defensive end Coy Bacon. By the season's end, Parrish and Bacon played a great deal, and Green was named Rookie of the Year. It looked then that Beathard had the Midas touch.

"I knew we had to get some players some way," Beathard explained. "I didn't really want to trade draft choices. I wanted to do it the way Dallas and Miami did, building through the draft. In most trades, you just inherit somebody else's problems. We don't feel trades are the answer, but we traded that first year out of desperation. We just didn't have any cornerbacks besides Joe Lavender. Parrish ended up playing in four Pro Bowls while he was with us, and Bacon, who was a throw in, played well for us."

The following year, 1979, wasn't too promising regarding the draft area. The famine continued for a second straight season when the Redskins had an NFL record low of five picks, and they weren't exactly the ones to build a championhsip on. The highest selection was in round four, and then it became progressively worse—seven, nine, eleven and twelve. It was a challenge that Beathard conquered. Three of the college players he chose, tight end Don Warren and linebackers Rich Milot and Monte Coleman, became starters.

If Beathard was feeling giddy before the 1980 draft, it was understandable. For the first time

Beathard: "When you're out scouting colleges like I did for so many years, you go to practices and watch coaches work."

since 1968, the Redskins had a number one draft pick. Beathard didn't hesitate to select wide receiver Art Monk, who went on to make the NFL's All-Rookie team. The same year, Beathard made defensive end Mat Mendenhall his second round choice. Like Monk, Mendenhall went on to become a starter. Slowly, Beathard was laying the cornerstone to make the Redskins a contender.

The turning point came in 1981. Realizing that 1982 wasn't that good for college players, he upgraded for 1981. Through some judicious trades, Beathard acquired a sizeable number of draft picks and used them wisely. Seven of the choices he made figured prominently in Washington's success the next two years. They included: tackle Mark May; guard Russ Grimm; defensive end Dexter Manley; defensive tackle Darryl Grant; wide receiver Charlie Brown; tight end Clint Didier; and linebacker Larry Kubin. His prize pick in 1982 was cornerback Vernon Dean.

It was not as easy as it appeared. Picking young players was one thing; developing them, another. After the 1980 season when the Redskins fell 6-10, Beathard had to make his convictions strongly known. This meant challenging coach Jack Pardee, and the success of the Redskins was involved. Beathard felt that Pardee severely hampered the progress of the younger players by sticking with the older ones too long. When he presented the facts to Jack Kent Cooke, the owner supported Beathard's analysis and dismissed Pardee.

After firing Pardee, Cooke went even further with Beathard in risking the Redskins' future. He instructed him to name a new coach, an area that had always been in the domain of the owner. In the back of his mind, Beathard knew whom he wanted. Not many people knew Joe Gibbs, who had been an assistant coach in St. Louis, Tampa Bay and San Diego. Beathard met him in 1969 when he was a line coach at Southern Cal and later at the University of Arkansas. Back then Beathard worked as a scout and was impressed with the way Gibbs directed his practices. Beathard convinced Cooke that Gibbs was the coach Washington needed.

"When you're out scouting colleges like I did for so many years, you go to practices and watch coaches work," Beathard said. "Once in a while a guy really catches your eye. This is how it was with Joe. Then I followed him when he came to the pros and kept hearing nothing but good reports about him. All through those years I said to myself that if I ever had to pick a guy to coach for me, he would be the guy I would go after. It was no gamble on my part because I knew what he could do."

The unwavering faith Beathard had in Gibbs was tested that very first season. The Redskins opened the 1981 campaign by losing their first five games. Beathard supported Gibbs all the way. When Gibbs turned the Redskins around and finished with an 8-8 record, Beathard was the first to give Gibbs the credit.

"This is where he showed everyone in our organization what he was made of," Beathard said. "He kept coaching, developing his staff and the players. He took the blame for their losses and never made any excuses. It was something to watch. The players realized they had some kind of a coach, even though they were losing. Joe was great. He never wavered. He was patient. "You know, you can get the players in here, but if you don't have a catalyst, a coach like Joe Gibbs, you are not going to be any better than the next guy. Somehow it worked. Joe had been preparing himself for this job."

So, too, had Beathard. He spent 19 of his first pro seasons as a scout. At first he tried to make it as a player and had more determination than anything else. As a 5'10", 170 lb. quarterback and safety at Cal Poly, he wasn't drafted. Ironically, the Redskins signed him as a free agent in 1959. He was cut and then tried to play with the Los Angeles Chargers in their first year in the new American Football League. Later he tried the Minnesota Vikings in their first season in 1961, but again did not make it.

"When I didn't make it as a player, I knew I still wanted to stay in football," Beathard said. "I didn't know exactly what I wanted to do. I thought about coaching, but then the chance came along in scouting."

This chance came through Don Kosterman, player personnel director of the Kansas City Chiefs. It wasn't much, only a part-time job scouting the college players on the West Coast. Although Beathard didn't have any experience as a scout, he wasn't exactly a stranger to Kosterman.

"He has always been a hustler and a guy with great drive," Kosterman said. "Bobby went to college out there at Cal Poly. That's where I first got to know him. My brother Tommy was on that team and another member of that club was John Madden. Bobby and John used to come down to the house on weekends, and that was how I got to know him. What later impressed me about him was the way he handled Mike Garrett for us at the time. Later, when Mike signed with us, he said how impressed he was with Bobby and the way he handled himself."

It was only the beginning. In 1966 when Al Davis left Oakland to take over as commissioner of the AFL to orchestrate an all-out war with the established NFL, he brought Beathard along with him to New York.

"I hired Bobby for the league office," Davis said. "We had the plan put together to take on the NFL. We had made him one of our area scouts. Scouting wasn't as important as signing. We wanted people who could take the stars we wanted right out of the NFL and sign them. That group was like a paramilitary outfit. We had them trained to move right in and make the moves. I signed all those guys to long-term contracts. That's so the NFL couldn't fire them. They had to be given jobs.''

Beathard went back to Kansas City three months later, remaining there until 1968 when he went to Atlanta. All those years he was on the road scouting. In 1972 when Don Shula, the Miami coach, wanted a player personnel director, Beathard was recommended. Although it meant spending less time on the road and more time in the office, Beathard joined the Dolphins. His admiration for Shula influenced his decision, and, besides, there were more beaches in Miami.

During Beathard's six years with Miami, the Dolphins won two Super Bowls. One eventually caused Beathard to resign, but he did so in a most unusual manner. Beathard took such pride in his scouts that he wanted to reward them with Super Bowl rings and raises, which owner, Joe Robbie, wouldn't approve. Beathard proceeded to put the names of the scouts on the league's waiver wire, which is actually used for player transactions. Surprisingly, several were hired by other teams at higher salaries. Beathard resigned soon after, getting the Washington job on a strong endorsement from Shula.

"Probably the greatest experience I ever had in football was working with Don Shula," Beathard said. "I would never be here now if it weren't for Don. I owe everything to him. When I took this job, Don told me I would have to buy some suits and get dressed up to go to work. I thought everything in Washington was downtown. I was very happy our office was out by Dulles Airport."

This makes it easier for Beathard to catch a plane as he still does a great deal of traveling because he strongly believes in scouting players himself. He goes anywhere at any time to look at a player and often looks at the ones no one else does. This is why he has had so much success in signing free agents. Nobody in the league has signed as many free agents as Beathard, but he doesn't do it just to add names onto the roster. Beathard sees talent in some free agents that others do not. As a result, there are more free agent players on the Redskins than any other team. It's not just luck, but design; it's Beathard's way.

"We had to be aggressive with free agents," Beathard explained. "We told players we would have a lot of positions open. We really tried to use it as a selling point. They could come in here and wouldn't have to compete against draft choices, but against free agents and veterans near the end of the line. There were a lot of players

here when I came in who were darn good players, but they were getting near the end of the line, and we didn't have a replacement system.

"That's why we had to depend a great deal on getting free agents. It's just a feel of things, getting to know the player well enough to know if you can count on him, seeing the little things he does. There are, for example, receivers with 4.4 speed and receivers with 4.6 speed. But can the guy run a route? Does he have the quickness to get open? Some guys get open without great speed. Can a cornerback with great 40-yard speed actually cover somebody? These are the things you have to evaluate. We do free agents differently from other teams, but I don't like to talk about how we do it."

In that regard Beathard is the catalyst. One time he went to his alma mater to scout a running back, Louis Jackson. He sent the player through a number of drills. One was a passing drill in which Beathard was the quarterback. He needed another player to cover Jackson running the passing route. The player turned out to be Mel Kaufman who ultimately impressed Beathard more than Jackson. Kaufman not only made the Redskins in 1981, but in 1982 became a starter as a linebacker.

"Mel caught my eye," Beathard said. "I told him he wouldn't be drafted, but we would sign him as a free agent. We gave him some money, and he was to use it to eat, to gain some weight before training camp. I told him, 'You will make the team.'"

Kaufman was one of many key free agents that Beathard discovered. Others include: guard Fred Dean; linebacker Neal Olkewicz; running back Ricky Claitt; center Jeff Bostic; kick returner Mike Nelms; tight end Rick Walker; wide receiver Alvin Garrett; linebacker Pete Cronan; running back Nick Giaquinto; wide receiver Virgil Seay; offensive tackle Joe Jacoby; running back Otis Wonsley; punter H. Jeff Hayes; defensive back Greg Williams; and cornerback LeCharls McDaniel. It was no wonder Beathard was the envy of the league. Still the modesty surfaced.

"Putting a team together is something no one person does," Beathard claimed. "The whole time a team is being put together, teamwork is practiced. Good organization is preached. When the team is successful, it bothers me when one man looks back and claims success for building the team. Even if I were the only person responsible for bringing in talented players, talent is only part of winning. We could have had the same players and not have done as well if the coaches hadn't handled the team right. And the players could have had the same talent and not have done as well without their work habits.

"With coaches who teach, all you have to do is bring them talented draft choices or free agents. With that combination, you don't have players walking out claiming they didn't get a fair shot. If a player doesn't make it with the Redskins now, it's probably because we blew it on the draft choice by not bringing the coaches a player with enough talent. One of the first things we did in Washington when Gibbs put his staff together was to have a meeting with all the coaches. We wanted to know exactly the type of person they wanted our scouts to look for. We didn't want our scouts looking for players that our coaches didn't feel were the right kind of guys. We wanted our staff members to work together without ego getting in the way. We have that."

The gut feeling that Beathard has about a player is perhaps reflected in the man himself. Never an outstanding athlete, he can more readily empathize with them. He can more easily transcend from the scout to the player, simply because he was there himself. John Madden, the colorful CBS commentator, thinks this is true. A close friend of Beathard, he roomed across the hall from him when they both played football at Cal Poly.

"It's like they say, people that were 'A' students don't make good teachers because they don't understand the people that have to struggle," Madden said. "As a player, Bobby always had to struggle. Anybody can pick out the superstar. He understands the smaller school kids. If you understand the marginal type, it's easy to understand the kid from the big school and the great player. Bobby doesn't rule out people until he's sure they can't play. That's the problem with computers today. They rule out too many players because of sheer numbers. Bobby will give the underdog a chance because he was one.

"He damn near didn't graduate from college.

Beathard admits his first few years in Washington were frustrating ones.

We had a class together. Bobby had left to go home and go surfing. I went to find our final grades. He'd flunked the course. I tried to call him to tell him he was in trouble, but I couldn't find him. He was on the beach somewhere. I talked to some people and got him a 'C' so he could graduate. When I told him, he wasn't even worried about it."

The course was political science. It figures. Beathard is a success in Washington without it.

"All I know is football," Beathard said. "I guess I've never grown up. It seems like I've never had a job."

Only blue jeans and sneakers.... ●

JOE GIBBS

"There Were Times When I Wondered Whether I Would Ever Become A Head Coach In The NFL"

As low key as he is, Joe Gibbs was beginning to wonder what it would take for his team to get respect. Even after the accomplishments of his Washington Redskins during the glorious Indian fall of 1982, Gibbs personally, and his team in general, still hadn't achieved the recognition champions usually get. Around the nation, and more precisely the kingdom of the National Football League, Gibbs and his band of Redskins were popularly known as the Rodney Dangerfields of pro football. The Dallas Cowboys, who were the only team to beat the Redskins during the regular season, weren't at all impressed with them even after Washington had defeated them for the NFC championship.

Even NFL Commissioner Alvin Peter Rozelle was somewhat guilty of not recognizing what Washington had accomplished. When he bestowed his accolades to Gibbs and owner Jack Kent Cooke following Washington's 27-17 victory over Miami in Super Bowl XVII, the usually astute Mr. Rozelle committed a faux pas. He praised Gibbs and his Redskins for having achieved the best record in the National Football Conference. The alert Cooke couldn't let the commissioner get by with that sin. His plucky Redskins had brought hope to every underdog in America week after week.

"My dear Pete," Cooke exclaimed, "we had the best record in the entire NFL!"

Rozelle broke into a sheepish grin and corrected his error.

Gibbs smiled, and he smiled the next day when a lady asked him for his autograph. He had just finished his early morning press conference on Monday, less than 24 hours after Super Sunday. He had hardly had time to savor the biggest victory of his brief coaching career. After he politely signed the slip of paper for the woman, she looked at the autograph and remarked, "Oh, I thought you were Don Shula."

The easy-going Gibbs wasn't the least bit offended. "See how quickly they forget," he laughed.

Yet, Gibbs probably wouldn't have it any other way. He is a low key, God-fearing man, who insists that his players kneel in prayer following a game to recite the Lord's Prayer. In a macho sport that is swollen with egos, Gibbs is subtle. It is refreshing, too. In the special Redskin Super Bowl Guide prepared especially for the press, a biographical sketch of Gibbs was missing. He wanted it that way. Other coaches would have been insulted. Gibbs seems to prefer the anonymity. Some insist on working that way, concerned only with the results, and Gibbs' personal scorecard speaks for itself. Washington lost only one game in the 13 times he prepared his team to play during the 1982 campaign. It was the best record produced by a Washington team since 1942 when the Redskins finished 10-1 and went on to defeat the Chicago Bears 14-6 in the world championship game.

When general manager Bobby Beathard hired Gibbs in 1981 to rebuild the Redskins' tepee, fans wondered, "Joe who?" Quietly, Gibbs assembled a coaching staff, rolled up his sleeves, and went to work. After Washington lost its first five games, Redskin fans blamed the team's poor start on the new coach in town, but Beathard had undying faith in Gibbs. When the 1981 season ended, a renaissance began. The Redskins won eight of their final eleven games with a squad laden with free agents and finished at 8-8. The most loyal Redskin fan needed a scorecard to identify his heroes much the same way Beathard had to identify his little-known Gibbs when he hired him after two years as offensive coordinator on the San Diego Chargers.

"I had done a lot of checking, and everyone said he was a winner," Beathard said. "It was just a gut feeling. When he lost the first five games, the team had every reason to fall apart, but he didn't let it."

It was an extremely crucial period for Gibbs. He not only had to prove to Redskin fans that he could win, but he also had to convince his players. The turning point came during an unscheduled late night meeting with quarterback Joe Theismann in Gibbs' home the same day the Redskins dropped their fifth consecutive game. From that point on, Washington began to build their winning program.

When he was hired, Gibbs merely promised to work his gut off, and that's what he did upon inheriting a team that had finished 6-10 in 1980. During the season, Gibbs slept as many as three nights a week at his office. He readily admits to being a workaholic, everything is a learning process with him.

"We take away something from each of our experiences, even losses," Gibbs said. "I learned a lot about myself when the team started off so poorly. I learned a lot about my coaching staff, too. We were 5-0 and I was just trying to survive, to hold on to a greased wall. I was just trying to win a game, just one game."

During those dark hours, Gibbs learned to be flexible. Although his quarterback was throwing well enough to win most of the games, the bottom line was that it all amounted to losses. Gibbs reasoned that his offense was not as explosive as the one he had developed at San Diego, one which was capable of overcoming mistakes. He felt that the Redskins were making too many errors so he changed his offensive philosophy. During those long night hours in his office, he rewrote the Washington game plane. He reverted to a high-percentage instead of a high-risk offense, one that was not conservative, but intelligent. The new quotient was a one-back system utilizing the strength of John Riggins' running ability, which was straight-ahead power, nothing fancy.

"We figured that if we could control the ball, not make more than two turnovers a game, run consistently and play aggressive defense, we could win," Gibbs recalls. "We could still take our passing shots, but we weren't going to succeed if we kept throwing 40 times every game."

Gibbs' success in such a short time, and in spite of an eight week interruption due to the 1982 players' strike, is a tribute to his coaching skills. However, it didn't come easy. He endured a seven-year coaching odyssey before he was finally considered head coach material.

His career began when he worked for Don Coryell as a graduate assistant at San Diego State in 1964. Gibbs went from there to Florida State, then to Southern California, and Arkansas, where Beathard first saw him. During those years, Gibbs was an offensive line coach. In 1973 when Coryell took over as head coach of the St. Louis Cardinals, he hired Gibbs as his backfield coach. The journey continued and in 1978 Gibbs was named the offensive coordinator of Tampa Bay. A year later he rejoined Coryell in San Diego as offensive coordinator of the Chargers; two years later, Beathard offered him the Washington job.

"There were times when I wondered whether I would ever become a head coach in the NFL," Gibbs disclosed.

Nevertheless, before he jumped at the chance with the Redskins, he met with Cooke. He wanted to get priorities in order, particularly his area of responsibility.

He was coming into a losing situation wherein Jack Pardee had been fired as coach after three years when the 1980 Redskins finished 6-10.

"I had a meeting with Mr. Cooke and went over just where I would fit in and what my responsibilities would be," Gibbs said. "There were certain things I wanted to have control over. He assured me I would have these powers."

What Gibbs was primarily concerned with in

The 1982 Washington coaching staff. Kneeling, from left, Bill Hickman; Warren Simmons; Larry Peccatiello; Gibbs; Joe Bugel and Don Breaux. Standing, from left, Dan Riley; Charley Taylor; LaVern Torgeson; Dan Henning; Richie Petitbon and Wayne Sevier.

redesigning the Redskins was final determination as to which players stayed and which went. He got it. He then clarified the working relationship with Beathard and they agreed on a system whereby the general manager would get the players who fitted Gibbs' needs. However, in the area of final cuts, which at times could be a delicate situation, Gibbs would assume full responsibility. If it came to keeping a free agent over a player who was drafted, Gibbs had the final evaluation. Gibbs was willing to risk his reputation on the players he wanted on the field. Beathard agreed with Gibbs' approach, and the two went about their mutual task of rebuilding the Redskins. Beathard, also, had a stake as he had risked his

reputation on Gibbs as the right coach.

"I never thought it was a gamble to hire Joe," Beathard said. "Everyone I talked to who knew him said he was an ideal head coach. There is something about him that makes him a winner. He is a fierce competitor, he's intelligent, and he has a way with players. Besides, people like Don Shula, Tom Landry, Vince Lombardi and Chuck Noll all came up through the assistant coaching ranks. Why shouldn't a Joe Gibbs succeed?"

However, no one expected Gibbs to succeed so quickly. In his first year, he brought the Redskins from a losing season to a break-even one. In his second year in Washington, before anyone really knew him, Gibbs reached the summit that

Running back John Riggins gets a tip from Gibbs.

some coaches labor for all their careers—winning the Super Bowl. Even Gibbs himself was astonished at what he had accomplished.

"There is no way I would've thought this would happen this year," Gibbs said. "I'm as surprised as anyone. Some 10 or 15 years ago, the guys coming into this business were allowed five or six years to build a program and get it where they wanted it. But I think those days are over. Now with society the way it is, people aren't going to wait. You have to get in and make it happen now."

It wasn't only winning the Super Bowl that finally earned Gibbs and the Redskins respect. It was how it was accomplished, thus confirming the outstanding job done by Gibbs. Except for Theismann, Riggins, and offensive tackle George Starke, Gibbs did not inherit a veteran team that could turn things around. Beathard brought in hundreds of players, mostly free agents and those cut by other teams, for Gibbs' final evaluation. It was simply a case of the right chemistry between players and Gibbs that made it happen. It was not the player formula of the standard NFL team.

Nevertheless, it worked.

"Our team is unusual," Gibbs admits. "We have a group of older players and a larger group of younger ones, rookies and free agents. There's little in between. They're 49 guys who go to work everyday and do their job. Some teams are really talented at some positions and dominate. We're different. We're 49 parts that fit together. After our first year, we evaluated things and sent our scouts out to find tough special-team guys, free agents, people who could think. There is no place on this team for players without intelligence. We tell our scouts that if college players they see can't think quickly enough, we don't want them. I'd rather have a 4.8 guy who can think than a 4.5 guy who can't."

In the week that the team spent preparing for Miami, Gibbs kept the atmosphere low key, much like his own personality. "We like the guys to have fun, as long as they know when it's time to get serious," he said. He didn't impose any curfews and told his squad to relax and do the things they normally did during the season. This philosophy was carried out right through to the

Gibbs diagrams a play for quarterback Joe Theismann.

A happy Gibbs makes a point at his press conference the morning after Super Bowl XVII.

Super Bowl.

Despite his intense nature, Gibbs appears calm and in control. He uses a commonsense approach with his players, and in return, his players find him approachable because like them, he makes mistakes. While others in his profession try to hide them, Gibbs admits a mistake if he's made one. In a coaching fraternity in which totalitarianism is the rule rather than the exception, this is a rare trait. His humanity is an extension of his religious beliefs as an acknowledged born-again Christian.

Religion is a very important part of Gibbs' life. While he is sincere in his practice of it, he tries to keep it as private as possible. During the players' strike, Gibbs conducted a Bible class for delinquent teenagers in Washington's inner city, and every Sunday morning he drove from his suburban home in Virginia to spend an hour at a program sponsored by a Baptist church.

"It was about the only positive thing about the strike," Gibbs said. "At least I was able to start working again with the kids on Sunday. It's something I really enjoy. When I was in Tampa, my church conducted a ministry with a local delinquents' home and I got involved in it and I really enjoyed it. When I came here, I told myself that I really wanted to get involved in something similar. During Sunday school one morning one of the members said he had some houses in the city, and he had contracted to open them up to these teenagers. He said he'd be willing to try a Bible class on Sundays if anyone wanted to help. It was like an answer to my prayers. We jumped at the chance.

"I don't want people to think that I'm trying to get publicity for myself or tell the world about myself. If I did, the kids may think I really wasn't sincere about it. But it's really rewarding for me. There is something about getting to know teenagers that I particularly like. They have great personalities. They are really sharp. They don't miss a thing. They just haven't had the experience we've had. And, they undergo a lot of heavy peer pressure at an age when they're making crucial decisions about what they are going to do."

The one thing that frustrates Gibbs is that he can't devote Sunday mornings to the kids during the football season or when training camp begins in July. Still, he thinks about other ways to help youngsters.

"Maybe a farm in the country where they could have a complete program, counseling, education, jobs," Gibbs said. "The aim would be to get them ready to go out into society and be useful citizens. I can see that happening down the road. I'm going to stay involved."

That is the softer side of Gibbs, but it is this involvement that makes things happen positively. At 42, he has the energy of someone in his twenties. The working part is one facet of his character, the teaching and motivating, the other. Gibbs taught his players how to win and motivated them into doing so with a soft but firm approach. His players know they can trust him.

"A lot of what I believe in comes from my association with Coryell," Gibbs said. "Most of all, I learned to treat people honestly and to admit error. When I was starting out I was very rigid, expecting things to be done in a certain way. But Coryell taught me to be flexible. What gets to a coach is that the situation is so highly competitive. What's toughest is when you go to a point and you've been somewhat successful and the next year you're not. Then what's said about you hurts your pride. The other thing is you work for six straight months with no days off—not a single day for the family.

"You build your own monster. What happens is when you aren't winning, people are saying, 'Hey, this guy, out.' When you start to win, then you are expected to win. You are always going toward one of those goals. Yet, when you win, all kinds of things start happening. First of all, you develop problems in signing players. Then, I think that you start believing that you are better than you actually are. You come back the next year with the attitude, 'We are the champs; we can't be beaten.' But, hey, just because you won some football games doesn't make you better in any way. You still get a test every Sunday, and in this grading you can't afford a C. It's either an A or you flunk. And two flunks could mean your season.

"It's still a challenge to me, and I'm not wor-

Gibbs gets a big hug from his father, Jack, after Redskins won Super Bowl XVII.

ried about burnout. What happens is, your pride gets hurt. You work so hard and then people don't think you are doing a good job. You get tired of that kind of thing. People write things, people say things, people say things to your children and that's what really hurts. You need to keep your priorities in order. I don't think football is the most important thing for me. I try to keep it behind God and family and friends.

"The players learned sometime early on this season that if they keep plugging away, good things will happen. Nothing came easy for them. They had to scratch and scramble every week. Now they believe in themselves, that they can win."

They did indeed. After defeating Miami in the Super Bowl, Gibbs was called a genius. He disdained the word.

"That idea is distasteful," Gibbs said. "It's embarrassing to me when people make that comment. I'm an average person. I work hard at my job, but there have been people in our business who have been at it for 10 years and have been really successful. Those are the people you should call successful. I'll never forget what Jack Kent Cooke told me. He said, 'Genius is the most over-used word in the English language.' The most exciting days of my life were, number one, the day I became a Christian, then the day I got married and when my two kids were born. This Super Bowl victory fits right in there. I feel kind of overwhelmed. Next year you have to prove yourself again."

For now, 1982 will do....

●

JOE THEISMANN
"Coach, I Think It's Time You And I Sat Down And Talked Because Something's Not Right"

A night light still burned in Joe Gibbs' home in the quiet Virginia suburb of Vienna. A few blocks away, Joe Theismann sat in his kitchen, talking with his wife, Cheryl. It had not been the best of days for either man. That afternoon before their hometown fans, the Redskins were defeated by San Francisco, 30-17. It was Gibbs' first season as Washington's coach, and it was his team's fifth straight defeat. Theismann had been removed during the fourth quarter of the game, something that hadn't happened in four years. Finally, at the suggestion of his wife, Theismann drove the short distance to Gibbs' home. Regardless of the hour, he felt it was time to clear the air.

Theismann was relieved that Gibbs was still awake. He answered the door, surprised to see Theismann standing there. Theismann wanted to talk, and the two did so for over an hour, finishing about midnight. Satisfied, Theismann left. Any doubts they had had about one another were removed that night. It was this summit conference between the coach and his quarterback that ultimately shaped the destiny of the Washington Redskins. A year later, they emerged as the world champions of football and, for the first time in his career, Theismann was recognized as one of the premier quarterbacks in the game.

At the time, however, Gibbs had reservations about Theismann. There seemed to be something missing on the field. Gibbs had brought a new system in from San Diego, which quarterback Dan Fouts had mastered making the Chargers the most explosive team in the league. Perhaps Theismann needed more time to grasp the philosophy of his system. And yet, Theismann was not doing badly on the statistical charts. He had passed for 599 yards in the first two games, but the Redskins still lost. Theismann was off to the best start of his eight-year career. Yet Washington was losing, and the Redskin fans were getting impatient.

Maybe Theismann was trying too hard. He had always taken on too much. When he first joined the Redskins he had volunteered to run back kickoffs. No one in the NFL remembered a quarterback doing that. He also held the ball on field goals and extra points. No one challenged Theismann competitively. Perhaps Gibbs also expected too much. Theismann was completely different from Fouts in temperament and ability. Both Gibbs and Theismann had to learn more about each other.

"I just walked up to his house at eleven o'clock at night and knocked on his door," Theismann remembers as if it were yesterday. "I told him, 'Coach, I

A Super Bowl smile.

think it's time you and I sat down and talked because something's not right, and I'd like to talk to you about it.' So we talked. We were 0-5, and that always lends some credence to doubt. But evidently Coach Gibbs had been misinformed about my feelings for the game of football. He was new in town and he had brought a whole new staff with him. Our owner, Mr. Cooke, had not been in the area that long so there was nobody there who knew me. All they could do was base their feelings on what they had heard about Joe Theismann. But it just wasn't true. I just wanted to clarify for him that football was the most important thing in my life.''

It wasn't so much Joe Theismann, the football player, but Joe Theismann, the off-field personality, that was the bone of contention. The irrepressible Theismann was a dominant personality in Washington. He was more well known than any congressman because of his active life. As an early morning radio disc jockey, and the owner of two restaurants in the area bearing his name, he was actively involved in charity work, had appeared in a movie, a television film, made countless personal appearances, and ultimately gave up a television sports show.

"It was a difficult time," Gibbs recalled. "I was looking at Joe and wondering how good he was. I was thinking, *Is this the guy you stake your career on? Is this the guy you want to be living with for the rest of your career?* I'm sure Joe was wondering just how smart we really were and what we really expected of him. Things were shaky, no question about it. We were both sitting back, not sure of what was going on.

"We discussed a lot of things, most of them personal. For example, Joe said he was concerned because a lot of people were talking about his outside interests and their effect. He wondered whether that bothered me. I told him, 'All I want is a quarterback.' I wasn't looking for a businessman. But he assured me his business would never interfere with his football, and it turned out right.''

The meeting took a heavy load off Theismann. He had been tight because he wanted to make things happen in a hurry under Gibbs' new system.

"I watched so many San Diego films that I was looking for blue-and-gold uniforms on the field," Theismann revealed. "I couldn't quite grasp Joe's offense. I had been taken out of the game against San Francisco. There was something missing between us. You couldn't put it into words. In essence, I got to know what Joe Gibbs wanted of me. We were doing enough things to win, but I was throwing interceptions and making bad decisions. He said, 'You just do your job and let the other guys do theirs.'''

Theismann settled down and was more relaxed and confident after his private talk with Gibbs. The Redskins began to win. They finished the 1981 season with an 8-8 record, winning eight of the remaining eleven games. Theismann's abiltiy to sit back and analyze what went wrong early in the campaign finally turned things around. He stopped trying to force the big plays, and Washington began to win.

"I forced the ball in 1978, but then I stopped," Theismann said. "Maybe the first couple of games this season, I was trying to force the issue and make something out of nothing. Instead of trying to make an impossible 20-yard pass on third and 20, it would be better to settle for a 10-yarder to give the special teams better field position. Learning Gibbs' system is not an overnight turnaround process. I thought it would come along quicker than it did. I was looking too deeply into the system instead of taking what was there on many plays. For example, on some of the interceptions I threw, I'd started to pass, reloaded and passed again. That's indecision. It was a matter of getting so familiar with the system that I run the plays naturally, not thinking about them. Now I can concentrate better on avoiding sacks and throwing the ball away on purpose. But it's hard to think of those things when you are concentrating so hard on the offense.''

Theismann had really needed that meeting with Gibbs, not only to evaluate his performance, but to assure himself that Gibbs wanted him as the quarterback. There had been suggestions that Gibbs might replace Theismann with rookie quarterback Tom Flick. Television commentator Moe Siegel said perhaps Theismann should be replaced if he didn't show more leadership and the team show more improvement. (The comments were made before the Redskins' fourth game of the season.) They rankled Theismann particularly because the remarks were made on WJLA-TV where Theismann was a sportscaster. Within 72 hours, he resigned his post, telling station executives he wanted to concentrate on football.

"I have had my share of criticism as a player and as a person," Theismann said, "and I've never stopped talking. But, I believe there has to be some credence and foundation to it. There was no credence and foundation in what was said. I didn't want to get into a situation where I had to worry about giving a rebuttal every Monday night to something that was said on the air. I felt it was in my best interest to terminate my employment.

"There's always been a list of knocks against Joe Theismann. They said I couldn't lead a football team into the playoffs. They said I wasn't tall enough to see over the pass rushers, or durable enough to take the hits. They said I was basically a scrambler who couldn't throw out of the pocket. They said I cared more for my own welfare than I did for my team."

No doubt about it. The early 1981 season had been a troubled time for Theismann and the Redskins. Theismann was playing with self-doubts. He was in the final year of his contract and had asked management to provide him with the security of a new one before the season began. But it hadn't happened. Some critics were blaming the club's poor start on Theismann's trouble with management. No matter what, the statistics tell the story. In the first five games, Washington's mistakes resulted in 11 interceptions and 10 fumbles, a total of 21 turnovers.

Theismann was hearing from the ghosts of the past. Critics drew comparisons with Sonny Jurgensen and Billy Kilmer, who were still regarded as heroes around Washington. For four years, Theismann had sat on the bench behind these revered veterans, waiting for his chance. After his meeting with Gibbs, he was more determined than ever. And the Redskins started to win, while the critics became less vocal with each victory. They won four games in a row, bringing their record to 5-6, only to see their winning streak snapped by Dallas. The beard that Theismann had grown over those weeks vanished.

"I had made a promise that I'd keep the beard as long as we won," Theismann said, "but when we lost, it had to go. I really didn't care for it, but

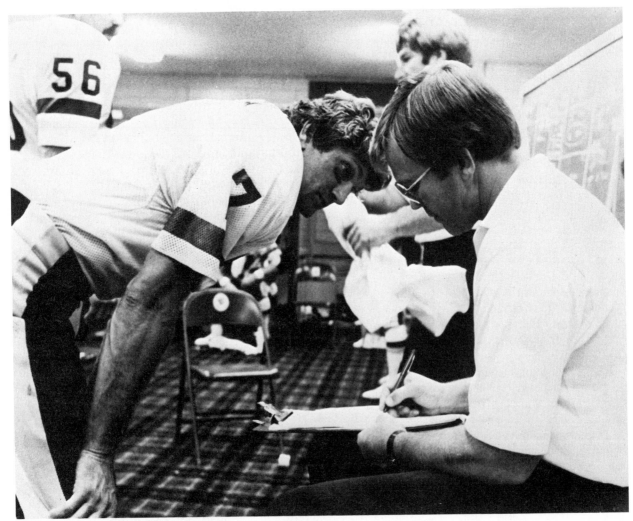

Theismann intently looks on as Gibbs goes over a point.

32

In 1982, Theismann enjoyed the best season of his nine-year career.

I was getting used to it—four straight wins. On some people beards look good, but I think mine made me look years older, and nowadays around here, you can' afford to look too old.''

There was a ring of truth to his jest. Theismann was thirty-two when the season began. He was a veteran on a team bursting with youth. Besides the transition involved with a new offensive system, he had to learn the nuances of younger, inexperienced players. Before the season came to an end, Theismann mastered it. He was enjoying playing football again.

"I'd liked to have played my whole career under this system," Theismann exclaimed. "God only knows what would have happened if I had. I have learned a lot in the past from people I played under, but this is one that's a quarterback's delight. It's versatile. The passes in it are not difficult. You have to take your keys and read them in order to execute the throws. If you do that in this system, you'll come out on top with the statistics to back it up."

As it turned out, the 1981 season was personally rewarding. Theismann had learned Gibbs' system so well that Washington finished with a flourish, winning their final three games. He overcame most of his critics and established a club record for pass completions with 293 and was second in all-time season passing yardage with 3,568.

Still, Theismann was somewhat of a paradox. He had never been selected for the Pro Bowl, despite the fact that in the final 1979 NFL quarterback ratings, he finished second behind Dallas' Roger Staubach. He still wasn't considered among the league's premier quarterbacks, and when it came to judging other Washington quarterbacks, he wasn't fully accepted as a star by Redskin fans. Theismann recognized it and hoped that time would overcome his detractors.

"Everybody in this town always retains memories of quarterbacks of the past," Theismann said. "You are never fully accepted. You just go out and do the job. You're always compared to Sonny, and that's going to go on for at least the next six years no matter who the quarterback is. It wouldn't even matter if you took the team to the playoffs or a championship. That's the way it is. Sonny is still a dominant and visible personality with his television appearances. People constantly refer to what he's done because his name is always up front.

"When things don't go well, there normally are two people who catch a lot of the heat, the coach and the quarterback. Conversely, when things go well, they get a fair share of the credit. It goes with the turf. That's part of being a quarterback. At the beginning, I took a lot of heat when we were losing. There was some criticism that I was upset because I didn't get the new contract I was seeking. I guess some people wanted to railroad me out of town, but when we came back, they didn't have anything to railroad me on. So they just sat and waited. That's the nature of some people in this profession. It was tough losing, sure, but the only reason we were 0-5 was because we were beating ourselves. It wasn't because we weren't a good football team or didn't have the potential. We just continued to make mistakes, but they were correctable. The things I did early in the year, for example, I knew were correctable. We just had to work hard and work ourselves out of it."

But what about the future? Theismann never hesitated. "We have a young football team with a lot of exceptional talent. Once it gets seasoned, it's going to be a real contender. That could be as early as next year. It's a football team that won't quit. We've proven that. It's a team that stays together through adversity."

It almost sounded as if Theismann were talking about himself. His career had been filled with adversity. At South River High School in New Jersey, he completed enough passes to Dallas star Drew Pearson that he had scholarship offers from some 100 colleges. Theismann was leaning toward North Carolina State.

"I got it down to four schools and three of them were in North Carolina," Theismann said. "There was State, North Carolina and Wake Forest. Actually, I would have liked to have gone to Duke because I like their colors. Little did I know that I couldn't get in there academically."

When a local sportswriter learned of Notre Dame's interest in Theismann, instead of praising the youngster he looked cynically at the 5'10" youth's chances of playing on the hallowed ground that was haunted by Notre Dame's heroes of the past. He wrote that Theismann would never survive as a 150-pound quarterback. The headline "Little Joe Will Get Killed at Notre Dame" angered Theismann. He tacked the article on his bedroom wall and decided that he would go to Notre Dame instead of North Carolina State.

"All my life I've been told I can't do things," Theismann said. "Either I'm too small or in the wrong place. If you want me to get something done, tell me I can't do it. What did I know about Notre Dame? I'm not Irish and I'm not Catholic and I'd never heard of Knute Rockne and George Gipp at the time. But, that was the wrong thing to say about me. When I finally showed up there, they had all these quarterbacks who were about 6'3" or 6'4", and you can see how tall I am. They list me at 6' but I'm closer to 5'10". But I just looked at it as another challenge. I decided that I was going to be the best of them all and be the best quarterback in Notre Dame history."

If he was to do so, he had to convince Ara Parseghian, the Notre Dame coach. He received his chance as a sophomore late in 1968 when he took over for Terry Hanratty, the regular quarterback who had been injured. Parseghian recognized some intangible qualities in Theismann that couldn't be found in statistics. Although he wasn't as big as other quarterbacks, Theismann was a winner. He was feisty and had charisma; the Irish players responded to his leadership.

Roger Valdiserri, the school's sports informa-

Theismann turns to hand off as Otis Wonsley runs past him.

tion director, had a special feeling about Theismann along the lines of the Heisman Trophy when he was only a freshman. The thought came to him quite spontaneously when he was attending a practice session.

"I was standing by some people at spring practice," Valdiserri said. "Joe went running by and somebody said, 'There's Joe Thees-man,' which is the correct pronunciation of his name. I said, 'No, it's not Thees-man; it's Thighs-man as in Heisman.' You could see even then that he was going to be a winner. He had all that electricity about him. Joe Doyle, a local sportswriter, printed what I had said the next day. But that was the last anybody heard of it for a couple of years. Joe was Thees-man until his junior year when a national magazine came to town, went through the clip files and saw the little thing Joe Doyle had written. They wrote it up, and from then on I called him Thighs-man."

Actually, Theismann was generating support for the Heisman Trophy. He led Notre Dame to successive appearances in the Cotton Bowl. As a senior, Theismann was one of the favorites in the Heisman vote. However, the 1970 trophy went to Jim Plunkett of Stanford; Theismann finished second.

"I remember sitting around the day of the vote, and the phone would keep ringing," Theismann said. "My wife was Roger's secretary, and she'd get all the calls coming in. I was doing well in the East, but Plunkett was carrying the West; the South was going to decide it all. It was like a damned presidential election."

Theismann was married shortly after graduation and he was anxiously awaiting the 1971 NFL draft. However, well before the draft, Theismann suffered a jolt. Shortly after Baltimore won Super Bowl V, the Colts' coach, Don McCafferty, said there were only four good quarterbacks in the upcoming draft, namely: Plunkett, Archie Manning of Mississippi, Dan Pastorini of Santa Clara and Lynn Dickey of Kansas State. He made no mention of Theismann. Apparently the other NFL coaches agreed. The criticism about Theismann was that he was too small. On draft day, three rounds went by, and Theismann's name wasn't mentioned. On the fourth round, Miami selected him. Computers are a way of life for most teams. Miami coach Don Shula didn't care what the computer read-out was. His own quarterback, Bob Griese, was only 6'.

"He's not too small," Shula said. "He's only half an inch shorter than Griese. We brought him into Miami. Joe came in and sat down with owner

Theismann didn't become a permanent starter with the Redskins until the 1978 season.

37

Only Sonny Jurgensen and Sammy Baugh have passed for more Redskin career yards than Theismann.

Joe Robbie and they came to an agreement. We called a press conference and announced he had agreed to terms and he went on TV, saying how happy he was to be a Dolphin. A week passed, two weeks passed and the contract didn't come back signed."

In those two weeks, Theismann figured out that he hadn't gotten all he wanted in the Miami contract. Instead, he received a better offer from the Toronto Argonauts and signed a three-year $150,000 contract, which made him the highest paid quarterback in the Canadian Football League. In his first season, he led Toronto to the Grey Cup Championhsip, Canada's answer to the Super Bowl.

"I was a misguided kid back then," Theismann acknowledges today. "I thought I was Joe Theismann of Notre Dame and that everybody owed me a living. I was wrong. Ultimately, the Dolphins worked everything out that we had talked about, but by that time I just became disillusioned."

After three years in Canada, Theismann wanted to return to the United States and play in the NFL. The Dolphins had won two consecutive Super Bowls and the thought of sitting on the bench behind Griese didn't appeal. Shula worked out a trade with George Allen, and Theismann signed with the Redskins for the 1974 season. In 1976 Washington gave the Dolphins the number one draft pick. Theismann didn't know it at the time, but Allen had a distinct preference for veterans, and not only that, he would be competing against Jurgensen and Kilmer, two popular players who were closer to forty than Theismann was to thirty. Theismann wasn't used to being a third string quarterback after having started the last five years.

"That time period was the toughest that I've ever gone through," disclosed Theismann, who felt that even returning punts was better than just sitting around doing nothing. "Herb Mul-key got hurt one day, and I just ran out there to return punts. I was going nuts. I was bored silly waiting for Billy or Sonny to get tired, and so I went out there. I loved it. It was during a Giants game, and I was standing next to George on the sidelines when Herb got hurt. I said, 'Coach, I'm going to return punts,' and he said, 'Okay.' Then when I

got out on the field, he started shouting, 'What's Joe doing out there?' But I was too far away for him to call me back."

After the 1974 season, Jurgensen retired. But there was still Kilmer. Even though he threw only 11 passes his first season with Washington, Theismann wanted to start. His rivalry with Kilmer was so fierce they never spoke to one another. It was almost to the point of being volatile. There was no question that the Redskin veterans backed Kilmer. He had Allen's support, too.

"Billy and I never got along," Theismann said. "It's no secret that we spent six months in the same room and never said a word to each other. After Sonny retired, it was all down to Billy and me, and that relationship I wouldn't wish on anyone. Week after week we'd sit in the same room and not talk. It wasn't antagonistic, just empty. There was no hatred. I don't hate Billy, and I

On the sidelines, Theismann points out something to running back Joe Washington.

don't even dislike Billy. I just don't have any feeling. I made it known to the press, and I made it known to Billy. I know I turned a lot of players off."

In 1975 Kilmer was still the starting quarterback. Theismann didn't get to play much more than he did the previous year. He managed to play only long enough to throw 22 passes. He played a bit more in 1976 and 1977. Still, Kilmer remained ahead of him. Theismann's frustration continued.

Then, a near-fatal heart condition to his three-year-old daughter, Amy, gave Theismann a new outlook.

"It all changed for me in 1976," Theismann disclosed. "My daughter Amy was in the Washington Children's Hospital. They discovered a hole in the upper two chambers between her heart. It was repaired with a patch. I can't spell what they called it. Just say they took out a dead battery and put in a super charger. She opened her eyes. She had an oxygen mask on her face, and she looked through it and said, 'Daddy.' One word changed my life. I realized the material things in the world are not important. Only to love and be loved are. It's to give, and not always to get.

"My situation in 1974, '75 and '76 is that I made statements I regret. A lot of my early problems were of my own doing. I came in and told everybody I wanted the job and made no bones about it. It didn't go over big with the incumbents. It immediately created a problem for me. As far as George Allen was concerned, I was never going to be a starting quarterback as long as Billy Kilmer was on the Washington Redskins. He had tremendous faith in Billy which remains to this day. I asked George to trade me, but he never did.

"Hey, I'd do anything to call attention to myself back then. If one play was called, I'd run around in the backfield and do something else and try to make a big play. I wanted people to notice me. I used to be for Joe Theismann a lot. I really used to try to see how I could make Joe Theismann more important. Now I don't think Joe Theismann is that important. It's the people I play with and my family who are important. I don't feel I have to prove anything. I don't feel Joe Theismann has to go out and make any marks for himself. If I do what I'm supposed to do, all those things will take care of themselves."

That's exactly what happened. In April of 1982 the contract that Theismann was seeking before the 1981 season was signed. It contained the security he wanted, four one-year contracts amounting to $1.5 million. Never having reached the playoffs, this was, nevertheless, the Redskins' way of showing faith. In 1978, he had displaced Kilmer as the Redskins' starting quarterback. At the end of that season, Kilmer retired. It was all up to Theismann and he didn't disappoint the Redskins. In 1979, '80 and '81, his performance steadily improved. In those years, he gave Washington the most consistent quarterbacking in more than a decade. And after all the years he had been in Washington, he approached the 1982 campaign with his best frame of mind.

"I thought we were one of the best teams by the time the 1981 season ended," Theismann said. "We've had a tough schedule and we're in a tough division, but I thought we were really having a good season. We really learned Joe's system and a lot of the young players were going to get better. I know I had a lot of fun playing last year by the time things were finished. What quarterback wouldn't be happy playing in a system where you pass so much? I'm convinced Joe Gibbs is going to be a great coach in this league and I want to tag along with him.

"There are a lot of people in this town who remember the accomplishments of Sonny and Billy, and rightfully so. But with Coach Gibbs taking over, the city has taken a whole different look at the Redskins. Under George Allen and Jack Pardee, we were looked upon as a defensive team, but we now have come full circle. Gibbs has opened up the game and has a totally different approach. We've moved from a Kilmer-Jurgensen town to a Joe Gibbs town. I ride the wave. Gibbs is the wave and I'm the surfer.

"Joe Walton, who was the offensive coordinator here, was the first coach to teach me to play quarterback. He taught me to play within myself. He taught me there were ten other guys on the field and that I couldn't do everything myself. You couldn't expect to make things happen on every play. That's when I first really began to understand what playing quarterback was all about."

Walton understood. He had the patience to work and wait for Theismann to develop before he left in 1980.

"When a quarterback starts out, so much is written about the bomb and striking quickly, they think they have to do it all themselves like some of them did in college," Walton says. "When a new coach or a new offensive coordinator comes in, they try to do the same thing, because they

Theismann: "I thought we were one of the best teams by the time the 1981 season ended."

want to make a big impression. I think that's what happened the first five games after Joe Gibbs came in, but then he settled down."

"It was a meaningful conversation," Theismann said, recalling his midnight conference with Gibbs. "We cleared things up. I love to play under Gibbs. Joe Walton liked to keep a governor on me; he was always afraid that I was going to run wild. But Gibbs loosened it up a bit and lets me run loose. We have a run-and-gun offense now, and we make things happen. I was comfortable under both systems, but I love the one I'm in now. Joe Gibbs stuck with me. He's given me more freedom, and he lets me do what I can do best. I'm a better player for that. If a player had the chance to play for one man in a lifetime, it would be for Joe Gibbs."

Theismann showed this during the 1982 season when, for the first time in his nine-year career, he became a playoff quarterback. He performed consistently. He finished as the leading passer in the NFC and was selected to play his first Pro Bowl. Despite an abbreviated nine-game season, Theismann completed 161 of 252 passes, a remarkable 63.8 percentage, for 2,033 yards and 13 touchdowns. He was efficient because he still had a zest for the game and played with the enthusiasm of a college star.

"I still have a little kid left in me," confessed Theismann. "I want to play football. I take a lot of pride in trying to outdo the rookies in camp. I try to out-run them, out-quick them. It's a little game that I started with myself a long time ago. My mental capacities are that of a guy who's played for 12 years, but my physical capacities are those of a man who's 22 or 23 years old. I condition myself differently than most people. I don't run. Instead, I condition myself in the kind of exercises I do on a football field.

"My personality remains consistent. I don't think I can hide my personaltiy off the field. I get excited. I jump around. I'm thirty-three years old. I watch my twelve-year-old son play football and when they score a touchdown, he jumps around. I have a thirty-three-year-old body, but a lot of twelve-year-old kid in me."

And, he certainly does. One Sunday befroe he left for the 1982 training camp, he treated his daughter Amy to a snack in a doughnut shop. He looked at her seriously.

"I told her, 'Daddy's leaving for camp tomorrow,'" Theismann said. "'Would you like Daddy to retire from football?'

"She said, 'No, I enjoy being the daughter of the quarterback of the Washington Redskins.' I thought to myself, 'Hmm, besides my own reasons, that's a pretty good one.'" ●

41

JOHN RIGGINS 6
"I'm A Mercenary With A Heart"

It was his greatest moment. John Riggins looked tired, and he had every reason to be. He had just established a Super Bowl record that may never be broken, and it was a performance from which heroes are made. There aren't many thirty-three-year-old runners in the National Football League. There certainly haven't been any in the history of professional football who did what Riggins did—carry the ball 38 times for 166 yards. Not ever. Super Bowl XVII belonged to Riggins. In a way, it was poetic justice. Riggins had stood alone all those years, and just a half hour after Washington defeated Miami 27-17, Riggins stood alone in a hot room with reporters from all over the country. He may never experience that adulation again, and he knew it when he said that tonight he was the king.

He has been called a great many things over the years. Perhaps the kindest description is that he's different, and even he wouldn't find fault with that. Riggins is difficult to get to know. Those who don't know him have referred to him as a flake, a kook and an odd ball—among other things. He is none of these. Riggins is perhaps the most misunderstood athlete in the NFL, not because of his ability, but because of his personality. He is a deeply sensitive individual whom few people understand or admire, a person with convictions who has matured over the years. There is still a lot of country in him, a great deal of the boy in his psyche, and he is at peace with himself in the quiet countryside of Centralia, Kansas. Riggins has always been a country boy first and one of the best running backs in the NFL second. He likes to do things his way, which often happens to be different from the other guy.

He was that way as a youngster; everybody around Centralia knew it. By the time he was a sophomore in high school, even people around the state knew it. But the football coaches at the University of Kansas didn't care. When coaches scout for high school talent and find a fifteen-year-old-who is 6'2" and 220 pounds of power, he could do anything. As a sophomore, Riggins was special. Don Fambrough, who recruited him for Kansas, was never bothered by the fact that Riggins was different from the next youngster.

"When everybody in the world cut their hair short, he wore his long," Fambrough said. "When everybody had long hair, he had a burr cut. I got my first look at John when he was a sophomore at Centralia High. I was down to recruit his older brother, Junior. The coach said, 'Follow me. I want to show you something.' We went to the gym and there was John pounding away on the basketball court. He was the finest physical specimen I'd ever

The many faces of John Riggins. In 1973 while with the New York Jets, he cut his hair in a Mohawk style, then shaved it off completely. Now, Riggins has a much more conservative look.

seen, and he was still three years away from graduation.''

When he went to Kansas, everybody in the nation knew about Riggins. He was All-Big Eight three times; All-American his senior year. He broke Gale Sayers' records with 2,706 career yards, and he never missed a game or a practice. In addition, even before he went to Kansas, Riggins was a track star. He was a two-time State 100-yard dash champion with a 9.8 clocking that wasn't overlooked by the NFL scouts. He was called a ''white Jimmy Brown,'' which was reason enough for the New York Jets to make Riggins their number one draft choice in 1971. It was Joe Namath's town, but Riggins cut his own path. He reported to the Jets' rookie camp wearing an Afro. He made coach Weeb Ewbank wonder by carrying an English umbrella, wearing overalls and a derby. Riggins was comfortable in a Greenwich Village walkup apartment which had a juke box and a barber's chair among other things. It was the good life. After signing a two-year contract at $25,000 a year, he began to learn about football life.

''Weeb said that he didn't want to pay for a pig in a poke, and I could understand that,'' Riggins said. ''A lot of number one draft choices never do

a damn thing in the NFL. But, I was as naive as they came. In college, I never realized I had KU over a barrel because of my talents. I was always downgrading myself. But I'm not a fool. It didn't take me long to realize I could play.''

Neither did others. In his rookie season, Riggins led the Jets in rushing for 944 yards. He would have easily gained 1,000 yards had he not missed the final two games of the season with an injured knee which was later operated on. Between that surgery and negotiations for a new contract, Riggins began to mature and acquire a new set of values.

''When we sat down in 1973 to talk about a new contract,'' Riggins disclosed, ''the first thing Weeb said to me was, 'Well, you didn't get your 1,000 yards.' Right then I realized the man had lied to me. He kind of tore my football soul apart. I realized then that this game was a business. He tried to make points against me, but I knew I had the Jets over a barrel as long as I was healthy. And I knew from what happened to Matt Snell that once you didn't have it anymore, there are no tears shed for you. You are a dead horse who's chewed up for dog food. New faces come in and the new man gets the publicity. It's life itself, the survival of the fittest.''

Riggins waits for a block by one of his ''Hogs,''

What Riggins wanted in salary was $150,000. Nobody on the team was getting close to that except Namath. Still unsigned, Riggins showed up in training camp that season with a Mohawk haircut. He didn't stay long. Ewbank refused to pay him the money. Riggins returned to Centralia and thought about quitting. Finally, he came back to the Jets and signed for $50,000 the first year and $75,000 the second. He wasn't happy about it.

"I had always wanted to play football," Riggins said. "But damn it, I never felt good about sticking my neck out and getting busted in half. The year before I had played stiff-legged, having no business on a football field, but playing because Weeb had come to me with those sad eyes. I'd played because I didn't want to let my teammates down. I had been overcome by my own peer group. But now I told myself, 'All righty, John, you have to do what's best for you.'"

In 1973, Riggins missed four games because of a sore shoulder and gained only 482 yards. The Jets missed him, too, as they finished last in the AFC East with a 4-10 record. However, in 1974 he again led the team in rushing with 680 yards as the Jets improved to a 7-7 record. Ewbank had retired and Riggins began a new round of contract talks with the Jets. Amazingly, he heard the same lament from management about not gaining 1,000 yards. Riggins couldn't believe it; he became angry.

"You could have put a match under me, and it would have lit," Riggins said. "I was that hot. I just didn't have to listen to that old cat-and-mouse game. I felt I was above that. I knew my talents and they should have known them too. They didn't belong in this business if they couldn't evaluate talent better than that. Right then I had my saddle bags packed. I knew I was going to leave after the 1975 season even though I hated to leave New York, which I loved. But, I knew what I could do, and I showed them my last year."

Playing out his option, which few players in the league did at the time, Riggins ran for 1,005 yards. The total was significant not only to Riggins personally, but because he was the first Jet ever to do so. He also led the team in receptions with 30, as the Jets hit bottom again with a 3-11 mark. Nevertheless, Riggins was voted most valuable player by his teammates. When talks about his 1976 salary began, Riggins didn't pull any punches. He demanded $425,000, the same figure Namath received.

"I had come to believe that I was as important to the Jets' offense as Joe Namath was," Riggins said. "He was their superstar and there wasn't room for anyone else. Namath was a little emperor. I can remember Weeb holding the airplane when Joe was a little late. That type of stuff doesn't create the atmosphere you like. A lot of veterans didn't say anything but then you may say Joe fed them the Super Bowl in 1969. But when I was there, I never saw him work one of his miracles. It's not a personal thing. Joe is a good fellow. I owe him a lot. I owe him for that thousand-yard season. In our last game he called my number 27 times and it took 27 times against the Dallas defense to get that thousand yards. I knew I wouldn't get his salary. It was my way of saying goodbye."

At 27, Riggins was a free agent. He still remained a free spirit in his dress, but he took on a completely new image when he met with several NFL clubs. This time he wore horn-rimmed glasses and a three-piece business suit, looking every bit the lawyer. He must have impressed Washington, because the Redskins liked Riggins and gave him a five-year contract worth $1.5 million.

Riggins was at peace. His five years with the Jets were a learning process, and it hadn't been an easy period. He had built up hostilities that were foreign to him and made him bitter. The boy in Riggins had become a hardened man. Life wasn't a game anymore. It was so cold, cruel and distrustful that Riggins often preferred to be alone. The Kansas countryside was his retreat. It offered him peace and quiet and a chance to think about priorities.

He reported to his first Redskin training camp at Carlisle, Pennsylvania, ahead of the other veterans. He wanted to learn George Allen's system, which was different from what he had done in New York. More than that, Riggins was happy again, and he wanted to play football. He got a lot off his chest that summer and was in a good frame of mind. There had never been any doubts about his physical condition. Everyone knew that Riggins was a football player.

"I'm a man of many different faces," Riggins said. "Shakespeare said life was a stage and we are all actors. I have a sneaky feeling he was right. Do you remember Tom Terrific in Captain Kangaroo? He used to sing, 'I'm Tom Terrific and I can be anything I want to be.' That's kind of the way I feel. I don't know if that's good or bad, but it makes my life interesting. I can always put on the right face to give people the right impression. I put people on the defensive. They are not sure what I'll do next. But if you scrape off all that outside stuff, down deep inside I don't know who I

Riggins looks for running room against the St. Louis Cardinals.

am, and I guess most people don't either.

"The Jets needed me if they wanted a championship, and, if they gave me what I was asking, they would have gotten every penny's worth. The ideal back can carry the football, block, run inside and out, and he doesn't make mistakes. On a scale of ten, I think I qualify around nine in all those categories. I don't think there is any other back in the league who can say that.

"For a couple of years I played the game without a heart. I was wrong and I apologized to the team for it. But I don't think any football player is paid well enough to risk permanent injury. I've gotten my head together now, and I think I'm more ready to play than I was three years ago. Still, you have to make a decision on how much you're willing to risk, and I think I know where my line is.

"I realized that all I had that kept me in the game was my machine. Just like a race driver at Indianapolis, if he blows his engine, he doesn't line up for the 500. By the same token, if I go out there and I blow my machine, I no longer have a job. It's a ticklish situation. The club always reserves the right to cut an injured player. Yet when an injured player holds back because he doesn't want to tear up his body, all of a sudden the ballplayer is a bad cat. I thought I'd help the team by staying out. If I was worried, I wasn't going to play well. Anyway, most of the time the Jets were out of the damn picture. I had a chance to be a truly fine running back and I couldn't see giving it up for one game when we were already whipped and were going nowhere.

"Still, I may have gone a little too far. I sat out when I shouldn't have. If I had been with an outfit that was shooting square, I would've taken chances. But all the Jets worried about was my having 1,000 yards so the press would have something to write about. Or, they worried about how many people Joe Namath would draw into a stadium. I never felt they were all that concerned about winning a championship in New York. It always seemed to me that it takes more than one man to win football games. But that was the way the Jet owners wanted it because they could make money out of it. That's what most owners are interested in, making money. Others, like Edward Bennett Williams, here, are more interested in winning championships, and that's why this year I'll risk my neck because I believe in Edward Bennett Williams.

"This is a game of machines. If a team has the machine and wants it to run, it's worth whatever they pay it to run. In New York the Jets got exact-

Joe Gibbs liked what he saw in Riggins in the months before

48

the 1982 season began. Gibbs felt Riggins looked sluggish during the 1981 campaign following his year's layoff in 1980.

Although he liked New York, Riggins wasn't happy playing with the New York Jets.

ly what they paid for. I didn't care about statistics after my second year. If I had put my mind to it, and if I had been on a team where they knocked down everyone for you, I would have had four thousand-yard years. But when the Jets set their bottom line, I set my machine at half-throttle. In football we are all mercenaries, whether a guy wants to admit it or not. This is like controlled warfare and no sensible body is going to do it unless the price is right. With the Jets I was a mercenary without a heart, but I think I've changed. I could have signed for more money with other teams, but I wanted to be with a winner. I'll stick out my neck this year because I want to be with a winner. I'm a mercenary with a heart.''

The heart wanted to run, but in Allen's I-formation, Riggins was used more as a blocking back. Allen's running attack was more halfback oriented, and Mike Thomas was the primary runner. Riggins still managed to gain 572 yards on 162 carries, an average of 3.5 yards a run. It was the

most yards by any Redskin fullback since 1971 when Charley Harraway gained 635 yards. At one point during the season, Riggins complained about not carrying the ball more.

"When I saw the Redskin films, I knew they had a tailback offense," Riggins admitted. "I came to the Redskins to help them win games, not to be an All-Pro. After I'm here a while, maybe it will change."

He was hoping it would change in the 1977 season. Riggins had big days in the final two games of the 1976 campaign. He carried the ball 19 times for 104 yards against the Jets. The following week he ran 23 times and gained 95 yards against the Cowboys. It strengthened his contention that when he was featured in the game plan, he delivered.

"People look at statistics when they talk about the best players, and sometimes that isn't the best criterion," Riggins said. "I figure I'm the best fullback in the NFL because I'm a complete fullback, complete with blocking. I may not get enough carries, though, to show a lot of yardage."

When Riggins reported for his second training camp with the Redskins in 1977, he remained strangely silent. It had nothing to do with his teammates. He decided that he wouldn't talk to any members of the press, and when asked why, he responded with a vague answer. "I was buried last year, let's just leave it at that."

It didn't turn out to be a good year for Riggins. During the fifth game of the season against Dallas, he hurt his knee and was through for the year. Little did he know that when he returned to Washington for the 1978 season, he'd find a new coach. Allen had left the Redskins after the 1977 season and was replaced by Jack Pardee, a former Washington linebacker, who had played for Allen in 1971 and 1972.

The change was beneficial for Riggins even though the Redskins missed the playoffs the three years Pardee was coach. In Pardee's system, much to Riggins' satisfaction, he was called upon to carry the ball more. He ran for 1,014 yards in 1978 and 1,153 yards in 1979, not showing any signs of the injury that had sidelined him during the 1977 season.

"This is the happiest I've been here," Riggins admitted before the 1978 season began. "This is the most relaxed camp Washington has had in my three years. The reason I feel good is the offensive changes that were put in. I was unhappy my first year here because I did more blocking than running. I had second thoughts about leaving the Jets. Last season, I missed half the year. But this year things are different. I go into each game knowing I'll get to run the ball. I wasn't happy my first season just being a yo-yo who had to concentrate on blocking.

"Coach Pardee liberalized the offense. We don't sit on the ball like we used to and wait for the other team to make mistakes. We go out and attack the other team now. Joe Theismann has also added another dimension to our offense. He's a good scrambler and can run for first downs. He's also becoming a leader on the field. My knee feels fine. I did a lot of running and lifted weights during the off season. I'm thankful I'm playing and carrying the ball."

The surprising thing about the 1979 season was Riggins' thoughts of retirement. A year before, he had carried the ball 248 times, the most in his eight-year career. Riggins was involved in just about half of the Redskins' total of 498 plays. He first spoke about his possible retirement in training camp just before his 30th birthday.

One season with the Jets, Riggins wore an Afro.

"One side of me says, play forever," he said. "Hell, if I wind up with a limp, I'll just go to the other side of the line and start chasing guys like myself. That's one side of my thinking. The other side says, 'Hey, look, you're in pretty good shape now. The knees are fine and you're not banged up. You've had so-so success. So maybe after this year, it's time to bail out.' It might be my last year. I've been thinking about it. That's what makes decisions, decisions. You've got to think about one side and then the other.

"If I hadn't had a good last year, I'd be with Chris Hanburger, Billy Kilmer, Jake Scott, Ron McDole and the rest. I'd be one of those fellows, a white elephant. At least, I'm sure, I wouldn't be a Redskin. In this business, especially at my age and with my salary, I'm only as good as my last game. It may not be what I decide, but what the season decides, if I have a bad year. But I've come to play. I'm looking forward to the year. If they want to give me the ball, that's fine. If they

Gibbs didn't like what he saw in Riggins in a 1981 game against Philadelphia.

want me to block, well, that's all right. When I signed, George Allen was the coach, and I didn't foresee any change. It hasn't gone the way you think. That's hindsight, but I don't think it was a mistake coming here. I'm perfectly happy in Washington. Everybody has a few regrets, but I've got too few to mention.''

The only regret Redskin fans had about the 1979 season was that Washington missed the playoffs for the third straight year. Dallas knocked them out in the last game of the season 35-34, by coming from behind in the final minute. Yet, Riggins had his greatest season with a career high of 1,153 yards and nine touchdowns. He finished the season as the league's ninth all-time rusher and didn't reveal any indications that he might be slowing down.

His performance encouraged Riggins to ask the Redskins to renegotiate the option year of his contract. He had one year remaining on his original five-year agreement that paid him $300,000, the highest salary in the club. He was willing to complete his final year at that figure. But, he wanted a one-year guaranteed contract of $500,000 for his option year. He felt if he were injured in 1980, he would be protected regardless for 1981. Owner Jack Kent Cooke, who at the time was overseeing the daily operations of the club, refused. Riggins threatened to sit out the season. When the Redskins didn't budge, he remained on his farm.

"Money wasn't the whole thing," Riggins said.

named the new coach, but Riggins still remained on his farm. It didn't take Gibbs long, however, to pay Riggins a visit. He told him that the Redskins would be happy to have him back if he wanted to play football again. If he didn't want to play, he wished him luck in whatever he decided to do.

"I remember when Joe came to the door," Riggins said. "I had a beer in my hand. I don't think Joe was pleased about that, considering that it was nine o'clock in the morning."

Riggins liked the way Gibbs came across. He recognized the new coach's sincerity and honesty. He appreciated the fact that Gibbs stopped by on his way back to Washington following the NFL meeting in Hawaii.

"It was a chance to talk for a couple of hours and gain some rapport," Gibbs said. "I told John I would help to arrange a trade to any of the four clubs that had expressed interest in him. At the same time I emphasized that I didn't want him back unless he really wanted to be a Redskin."

Although Riggins made it clear to Gibbs that he didn't want to be traded, he also remained non-committal about coming back for the 1981 season. Several months later in June, Riggins showed up at the Redskins' mini-camp.

"I think that meeting helped," general manager Bobby Beathard said. "Once he met Joe face to face I knew John would like him."

Apparently, Riggins liked what he saw in a new era of Washington football. He reported five days early to training camp that summer. He didn't regret his decision to sit out a year.

"I'd advise any player to take one year off," Riggins said. "It gives you a chance to reflect. Some guys probably wouldn't come back, but I wanted to. I found life kind of boring without football. I'm broke, I'm bored and I'm back. I'm really here to play football and not to do a lot of talking."

He didn't either. Politely but firmly, Riggins refused all interviews that summer. The silence lasted almost until the end of the 1982 season. When the 1981 campaign began, Riggins got off slowly. There was some talk that after a one-year layoff, and at the age of 32, he might be finished. It wasn't until the fifth week of the season, when Gibbs installed his one-back offense, that Riggins began to show his old form, finishing the year with 714 yards rushing.

"Going into our third game of the season with Philadelphia, he played very poorly," Gibbs said. "He hadn't shown much and in Philadelphia, he

"It was part of it, sure, but it wasn't the whole thing. I had gotten to a point where football wasn't fun anymore. We had just lost our last game to Dallas and that took a lot out of me because I thought we had a pretty good shot at the Super Bowl. Then I saw former players walking with a hitch in their gait and I realized that could be me someday. I still had two good legs and it seemed if I was ever going to get out that was as good a time as any."

That fall Riggins painted his house and never ran a play for the Redskins. He was missed. In 1979, he was half the team's offense. Without him, the Redskins had a void they couldn't fill. Super Bowl hopes crashed. The Redskins finished 6-10 and Pardee was fired. Gibbs was had a very bad game. I thought maybe he was finished, that the year had taken too much out of him. I had been looking for all the good things I had been told about. The coaches thought John would play better than he had or he was probably through. I think John thought so, too."

Before the 1982 season began, Riggins talked with Beathard about his contract. He was in the option year of the five-year contract he signed in 1976. One thing Riggins wanted to avoid was a salary dispute. By playing the option year at his original salary, he would be automatically entitled to a 10 percent increase and earn $330,000.

"John told me he didn't want to go through the negotiation hassle," Beathard said. "He said that we probably wouldn't pay him any more than his option year salary anyway, so why not just settle for that."

A determined Riggins didn't want to settle for a mediocre season. He had too much pride. He prepared for the 1982 campaign with a difficult training camp, working harder than ever on a weights program. It made Dan Riley, the team's new weight and conditioning coach, rave about him.

"He has worked as hard as any Redskin on the weights," Riley said. "Nobody at camp spent more time working on them. He'd be going through his program three times a week even when we were having two-a-day practices. I'm not talking about easy stuff either. I push him hard, very hard, and he keeps coming back for more. John is an intelligent guy. I guess what we said made sense to him. But you can't force anyone to come in here and work. He's done it on his own."

After the pre-season round of four games, Gibbs was impressed with Riggins. It fortified his theory to build the offense around him.

"Last year, he was affected by the year's layoff, no question in my mind about that," Gibbs said. "He's like a different runner this summer. He was sluggish, now he's strong. But it's more than that. He looks strong and quick, the quickest I've seen him. I told John he would have to carry a load for us. But he's going to set his own path in life. I think he prides himself in doing things a little differently."

Riggins didn't mind the heavy load placed on his shoulders. He thrives on that. He has to feel needed, wanted. When he does, he responds. That's all the incentive he needs.

"I'd like to carry a lot," Riggins said, "because it takes time to get my rhythm. I don't thrive on

work. But I know what I have to do on Sunday, and I know what I have to do during the week to be able to do it on Sunday."

During the 1982 season, the first players' strike in league history interrupted Riggins' rhythm. It wasn't until the playoffs that the noise grew louder and louder each week, reaching a crescendo in Super Bowl XVII. Riggins set records in the playoffs and the Super Bowl that may withstand time itself. It was his first appearance in the post-season tournament and the Super Bowl drove him like no other time in his 11-year career. He gained 444 yards in the three playoff games, finishing with 166 in the Super Bowl. To many running backs, that's a complete season. Riggins gave no indication that he felt any Super Bowl pressure, even though the Miami defense was waiting for him.

He appeared loose at one of the daily press conferences, not only chiding the large press corps, but Gibbs as well. He followed Gibbs to the microphone and actually enjoyed himself with some classic remarks.

Q. Did you gain a new perspective being out of football for a year?

A. Yeah, I gained a new perspective through the eyes of my banker. (Translation: He missed the money.)

Q. Where did you spend that year? In the mountains?

A. In Kansas?

Q. What do you attribute your longevity to?

A. Formaldehyde.

Q. Was Joe Gibbs the main reason you came back?

A. I would have played somewhere. But it would have been difficult for me to continue with the Redskins if it weren't for Joe.

Gibbs looked up. "I'm listening, John," Gibbs exclaimed.

"Just remember, Joe," Riggins said. "When you came to see me in Kansas last year, I told you you were gonna be a great coach, with or without me. So far, you've proved half of that."

A couple of days before the game, Riggins put it all in perspective in a more serious tone.

"What does the Super Bowl mean?" Riggins asked. "An opportunity to fulfill a dream. Other than that, just another football game. But this atmosphere is so extraordinary, it's not an ordinary work week. It's like astronauts about to take off on a space shuttle. It may not hit them until they get in the shuttle, but it will then. This will hit me the same way."

Miami certainly found out.... ●

DAVE BUTZ

"I'd Give Up All-Pro For A Team, A Defensive Unit That Wanted To Be The Best It Could Be"

It took him a long time to win recognition. He had played the game for ten years, and finally in that glorious season of 1982, Dave Butz was appreciated. Still, he didn't get the All-Pro honors that many felt he deserved and that hurt because Butz had had the best season of his seven-year career as a dominant tackle on Washington's defensive line. He led other linesmen in tackles for the second straight year. Anyone could understand those statistics because Butz is 6'7" and weighs 295 pounds. However, he has told critics for years that statistics aren't everything.

In the trenches where the real war occurs every Sunday, statistics don't mean a thing. No one watched what was actually going on. There weren't any points given for beating down on two or three blockers at a time, or plugging the hole on the bottom of a pile to cut down a running play. Maybe people expected more of Butz because he was so big. For example, picking up blockers and throwing them aside and grabbing a quarterback and sacking him for a ten-yard loss all in one play. But it just doesn't happen that way.

Butz is steady if not spectacular. The best praise one can give him is that he is consistent. This was essential since the Redskin defensive line limited opposing offenses to 101.2 yards rushing per game in 1982. Perhaps if he were more flamboyant, jumping up and down with both arms extended in the air, he would have been noticed more easily. It's not his style. Butz is a quiet giant. If he were more outward and controversial, he might have made the Pro Bowl roster years ago. It had to be frustrating to him, although he won't admit it.

"I don't really feel I've been playing any differently than I have in past years," Butz said. "But to get the notoriety, you have to have people watch you, because statistics don't tell the entire story. They don't say if a guy is double-teamed, or if a pass is tipped before it's intercepted. Someone has to be watching you all the time, and not many people do that. When the Pro Bowl ballots came out, I told myself I wasn't going to let it worry me. I wasn't going to think about it. That's how it came out and there was nothing I could do about it.

"I've had head coaches in team meetings say, 'This play depends on Dave Butz' taking two guys.' It puts a helluva lot of pressure on you. The average person doesn't know that and doesn't recognize it. But that's what they said. You're only as good as the people you associate with, whether by choice or design."

Butz was the biggest thing to hit the NFL since the pro football league

St. Louis quarterback Neil Lomax feels the weight of Butz.

merger, and the St. Louis Cardinals believed it in 1973. They selected him on the first round, the fifth player taken out of the 440 or so picked in the college draft that year. Butz was heavier when he attended Purdue University. He weighed almost 15 pounds more, but it wasn't unusual for him. He had always been big.

Born in 1950, he measured 24 inches. His parents told him he cried a great deal after being fed. After weeks of exasperation, they cut the tip off the bottle, allowing a wider opening so that strained meat could come out with the milk.

At three, his father placed him behind the wheel of a two-ton truck. He pitched hay from the back while his son steered. In kindergarten, Dave stood eye to eye with his teacher. By the time he reached fourth grade, Butz weighed 150 pounds and frightened the smaller kids.

As a teenager, he was 6'2" and weighed 230 pounds. When he played football at Main South Park High School in Park Ridge, a suburb outside of Chicago, Butz was 6'6" and weighed 265 pounds. He became so carried away during a pre-game warm-up for a basketball game that he shattered the glass backboard when he dunked the ball.

He didn't have any doubts about attending Purdue. His uncle, Earl, the former Secretary of Agriculture, was dean of the School of Agriculture.

"People don't realize that I work as hard or harder than anyone," Butz said. "One game in college, I was blocked by four players. I would fight through them but there'd be no reward at the end. The quarterback and the ball carrier would be gone."

The Cardinal scouts were impressed with Butz, and the year he was drafted, they passed up Chuck Foreman, Isaac Curtis, Wally Chambers, Otis Armstrong, Darryl Stingley and Charles Young. That was the easy part. After Butz was selected, his attorney, Arthur Morse of Chicago, reached a salary impasse with the Cardinals. By the time it was resolved, Butz had missed preseason training camp. Nevertheless, he still made the league's All-Rookie team. In 1974 a players' strike disrupted Butz's progress. He suffered a further setback when he injured his knee in the opening game of the season. As a result, he was unable to play again that year.

Butz was one of ten Cardinals who played without a contract. He wanted to remain with the

A rare moment for a defensive lineman. Butz intercepted a pass and ran to the one-yard line before being tackled in a 1981 game against Chicago.

The Redskins gave up three draft choices to St. Louis, two number ones and a number two, when they signed Butz as a free agent in 1975.

Cardinals, but couldn't come to contract terms with Joe Sullivan, the team's general manager. On May 1, Butz was officially a free agent. The Redskins and the Oakland Raiders both expressed an interest in him and began negotiating with the Cardinals.

Even though Butz signed with Washington on August 5, the contract was still not complete. Although Sullivan had regular contact with George Allen, an agreement for Butz could not be reached. Rather than take the case before Commissioner Pete Rozelle, Washington owner Edward Bennett Williams met with St. Louis owner Bill Bidwell. An agreement was reached in early September. The Redskins paid a high price for Butz, a number one draft choice in 1977 and 1978 and a second round pick in 1979. Despite the fact that he called Butz "potentially the best defensive lineman in football," Sullivan, who worked for Allen in Washington several years before going to St. Louis, had pulled a fast one on his old boss.

Butz was happy to sign with the Redskins, but his experience with the Cardinals left him bitter.

"They just plainly said I wasn't worth very much because they didn't know what I could do," he said. "All down the line they questioned my ability as a player. As soon as I signed with the Redskins, they said they had lost one of the greatest football players ever. Before I was nothing, but I do feel maybe the Cardinals got a little too much for me, even though these are pretty distant draft choices. The good thing about the whole deal was that the Redskins didn't have to give up a player. I was very concerned about that, because it would have some serious implications. I knew what a close group the team was, and I didn't want to have that broken up at my expense. That's what worried me the most."

Butz was observant from the beginning. Washington was still happy with Allen's "Over The Hill Gang." For Butz, it meant Allen preferred Ron McDole, Verlon Biggs, Diron Talbert, Bill Brundige, Manny Sistrunk and a few other veterans. When he joined the Redskins, a month after training camp began, he still lacked valuable experience, especially under Allen's system. He had played only one year of professional football and was still a rookie. He wasn't even sure where he would be asked to play.

"I think, ultimately, the position I'll probably be at is tackle," Butz claimed. "I think it's where I belong. Because I'm so big, it's kind of hard for people to root me out. If I get down and tee off, well, there's nobody one-on-one who should be able to put me in a position to take me out of a play."

He had to wait. He didn't play much in the 1975 season, but the Redskins finished 8-6. He wanted to play, to contribute, to prove he was worth the big price the Redskins paid for him, but he resigned himself to the knowledge that Allen depended on his veterans.

"Sure there's pressure on me to produce," Butz admitted. "The deal caused me a little problem with the other players. I've put pressure on myself. The Redskins gave up a lot to get me. All I want is a chance to help the team, to do my best. I really like it here, though. George Allen is defense-minded, which I like, of course. He is dedicated to winning and he is scientific. He really researched me, even down to watching my college films.

"When I first went to the Redskins, Coach Allen told me he expected a lot out of me and that he would be using me more as the season went on. He also told me to improve my physical and mental condition. When I first came here, I weighed 303 pounds, but now I'm down to 287. I'm probably in the best shape I've been in since college. I'm learning and I'm going to play a lot later on.

Butz' primary objective is to stop the run.

"The big difference between the two teams is that there's a lot more real pros here. The feeling here is that anytime, we can make anything happen. I've never seen so many statistics; we're given every type of scouting report there is. In St. Louis we watched the films and that was about it."

The first year with Washington was a learning process for Butz. He returned to training camp in 1976 with a brighter outlook. It was his first full training camp despite the fact that he was beginning his fourth year as a pro. His opportunity to play brightened considerably when Sistrunk was traded to Philadelphia. Butz was still tormented by the high price over his head.

"Two number ones and a number two," Butz sighed. "It astonished me when they did it. It still does. I've got a lot of work to do to justify what they put out for me. Under Coach Allen you have to play errorless football. I'm still too slow off the ball. I have a tendency to rise up and look into the backfield, instead of getting rid of the guy in front of me first and then worrying about reading the play. It would make it a lot easier to handle him instead of giving him time to get set.

"The main thing is that I'm trying. I'm trying to get better and improve. I'm not playing as well as I should, but I can see improvement. That's encouraging, but when you're not producing and you want to produce, it's hard not to get down on yourself. Coach Allen pointed that out to me. But I want to play better and sometimes I get impatient. I know the fans are watching me closely to see if I am playing as well as they think I should."

Butz pushed himself. He worked harder than ever the eight weeks he spent in Carlisle getting ready for the regular season. He lifted more weights, ran more laps and watched more films than ever before. He was down to 282 and by his own admission was in "the best shape of my life."

LaVern "Torgy" Torgeson, the Redskins' defensive coordinator, was pleased with Butz' work habits.

"We can see progress every week," Torgeson said. "He's coming off the ball better, and he's got our defenses down well enough so he doesn't need to think anymore, but just react. I think he can develop into the player we want because he already is good against the run and knows he needs to work on pass rushing."

Still, Butz wasn't a regular when the season began. Although he played more than the previous year, it was not enough and critics intimated he was not helping the team. Butz felt most of the

Butz, with help from linebacker Brad Dusek, brings down St. Louis running back Ottis Anderson.

63

hostility came from his own teammates. The compensation the Redskins paid and Butz' three-year $210,000 contract still gnawed at some of them. Off season, Butz worked hard. He voluntarily attended a three-day mini camp in the spring of 1977 with free agents and draft picks.

"I've always had the motivation," Butz said. "Coach Allen is providing every player on the team and even those who aren't on the team a chance to come in here and to better themselves. If people don't show up to do so, then they're hurting themselves, and they're hurting others."

When the 1977 season began, Butz again resigned himself to a reserve role. Allen stayed with the veterans even though they were a year older. Since the Redskins made the playoffs the year before with a 10-4 record, he felt he could get one more season out of them. However, it didn't happen. Although the Redskins won the final three games in a row, they finished with a 9-5 record, which was not good enough to make the playoffs.

At season's end, the structure of the Redskins changed dramatically. Allen left to coach the Los Angeles Rams and Bobby Beathard was named general manager of the Redskins on February 24, 1978. Jack Pardee was hired as coach and Butz' career was about to make a dramatic change.

Pardee was familiar to Redskin fans. He had ended his playing career as a linebacker with Washington in 1971-1972. He changed Washington's defensive front from a 4-3 to a 3-4. Because of his size, Butz was given the opportunity to play nose guard, the main function of which was to exert pressure on the opposing center and stop the run. It was a new challenge, and he accepted it with the realization that finally he had an opportunity to become a starter. He performed so well that he was voted the Redskins' defensive player of the year.

"Coach Allen played the veterans as much as he could," Butz said. "It was hard breaking into the lineup ahead of Bill Brundige and Ron Mc-Dole. Those guys had played together for five years and had their own personal signals. Because I didn't catch their signals all the time, I'd be left out in the blue. However, the thing about the 3-4 is it makes for some long, frustrating days. They double-team the guy over the nose all the game. You actually can get hit by seven or eight different people, either the tackles, the guards, the center or any of the backs."

In 1978 Butz played more than any other defensive lineman and was held more by opposing linemen. Everytime he left the field his shirttail hung outside his pants. He thought he could remedy the situation to some degree by tapering his jersey at the end.

"You're not a good player if you're not being held, I guess," Butz reasoned.

Butz finally showed how good he was. From that season on, he became an integral part of the Redskins' defensive line. When Joe Gibbs took over as coach in 1981, Butz had already established himself. It was the third coaching change he experienced in his seven years with the club, but he'd never been happier.

"The 'Over The Hill Gang' was a very cliquish group," Butz said. "They did a lot of things together on and off the field and it wasn't easy breaking in. It was frustrating sitting on the bench the first couple of years. Then when I knew the audibles, when I heard them in games and saw them in writing, they couldn't mess with me anymore. That's when I excelled. That's when I went past them like a comet, because they were so old they got double-teamed, were so weak they couldn't do it anymore.

"I love people who have the willingness to learn, people who have a quest, a thirst for learning, people who want to be better, to improve themselves. I'd give up All-Pro for a team, a defensive unit that wanted to be the best it could be, that got after somebody, that played the defenses that were called superbly. That's what we're trying to do here."

He certainly sounds like an All-Pro. ●

Butz: "I don't really feel that I've been playing any differently than I have in past years."

1982 SEASON
"I Don't Think What We Did At The End Of Last Year Was A Fluke"

The strong finish in the final half of the 1981 season gave Gibbs a confident feeling about the 1982 campaign. In the months before training camp, he felt strongly about the fact that the Redskins could improve upon their 8-8 record and even talked about making the playoffs. Gibbs was looking for improvement from a young offensive line that was rebuilt at the start of the 1981 season. He was also looking for a stronger defensive showing, namely a better pass rush and consistency in defending against the run. Although the team had won eight of its final eleven games, there were skeptics who didn't put much weight into Washington's chances for 1982. Nevertheless, Gibbs' confidence never waned.

"I don't think what we did at the end of last year was a fluke, but we still were only a .500 team that needed to do a lot more improving," Gibbs said at the start of training camp in Carlisle, Pennsylvania.

"The most rewarding thing about last season was that we found we had players who just wouldn't quit. They kept heart and just kept fighting and scrapping and believing in themselves."

It began with Theismann, who was the catalyst of the offense. After the team's shaky start in 1981, Theismann never became discouraged. Like everyone else, he had to maintain confidence in Gibbs' offense. Even though the Redskins were losing, Theismann felt the players were performing well. He knew it was a matter of time before the team would start winning. At the end, Theismann had the best season of his eight year career with Washington.

"For the first five weeks, we were changing everything every week—calls, formations, players, what have you," pointed out Theismann. "I thought we were one of the best teams by the time the season finished."

The best receiver Theismann had was Art Monk. General manager Bobby Beathard hadn't hesitated for a moment in making the swift wide receiver his number one draft pick in 1980. That alone earned Monk special status even before he walked on the playing field. The former Syracuse star was Washington's first number one draft choice since 1968. In 1981, Monk's total receiving yardage of 894 was the most achieved by anyone since 1967.

Washington's opponents also realized how good Monk was and double-teamed him. It was one of the problems Gibbs was concerned with during training camp. He was hoping that Charlie Brown, another swift wide receiver, would have a good pre-season after being sidelined for the entire 1981 campaign with a knee injury. Although he was only 5'10" and considerably short-

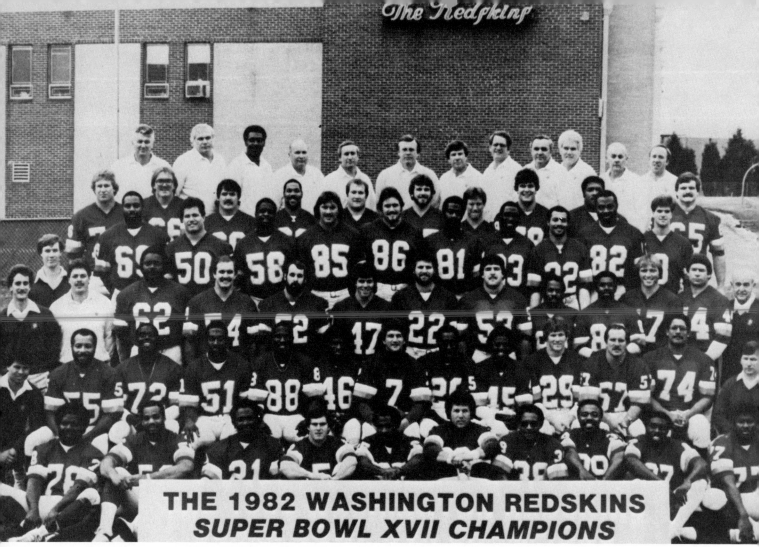

THE 1982 WASHINGTON REDSKINS
SUPER BOWL XVII CHAMPIONS

Front Row (left to right): DE Tony McGee, LB Quentin Lowry, KR Mike Nelms, P Jeff Hayes, RB Joe Washington, K Mark Moseley, RB Clarence Harmon, RB Otis Wonsley, WR Charlie Brown, and DT Darryl Grant. Second Row: Assistant trainer Keoki Kamau, LB Mel Kaufman, DE Dexter Manley, LB Monte Coleman, TE Rick Walker, CB LeCharls McDaniel, QB Joe Theismann, CB Joe Lavender, CB Jeris White, FS Mark Murphy, LB Rich Milot, T George Starke and trainer Bubba Tyer. Third Row: Equipment manager Jay Brunetti, assistant strength coach Jim Speros, T Donald Laster, LB Peter Cronan, LB Neal Olkewicz, FS Greg Williams, FS Curtis Jordan, C Jeff Bostic, WR Alvin Garrett, WR Virgil Seay, QB Tom Owen, RB John Riggins, assistant trainer Joe Kuczo. Fourth Row: Assistant equipment manager Stretch Williams, DT Perry Brooks, LB Larry Kubin, LB Stuart Anderson, TE Don Warren, TE Clint Didier, WR Art Monk, SS Tony Peters, CB Vernon Dean, TE Rich Caster, and QB Bob Holly. Fifth Row: DE Mat Mendenhall, T Joe Jacoby, G Russ Grimm, G Fred Dean, T Garry Puetz, DT Pat Ogrin, RB Nick Giaquinto, DE Todd Liebenstein, T Mark May, and DT Dave Butz. Back Row: Special Teams Coach Wayne Sevier, Defensive Coordinator Richie Petitbon, Receivers Coach Charley Taylor, Defensive Line Coach LaVern "Torgy" Torgeson, Linebackers Coach Larry Peccatiello, Head Coach Joe Gibbs, Offensive Line Coach Joe Bugel, Assistant Head Coach Dan Henning, Tight Ends Coach/Offensive Scouting Warren Simmons, Running Backs Coach Don Breaux, Administrative Assistant and Defensive Scouting Bill Hickman, and Strength Coach Dan Riley.

er than the 6'2" Monk, Brown had 4.5 speed, which was just a fraction higher than Monk at 4.4.

"Charlie has a way of gliding and then turning on the burners," said Beathard, who drafted Brown on the eighth round in 1980. "He's deceivingly fast and he has good hands. I think last year brought up a question about his toughness. The injury really affected him mentally. Fortunately, he benefited from the experience. If he's ever hurt again, I don't think it will get him down nearly as much."

In the off season, Brown worked hard rehabilitating his knee. He also started lifting weights which made him stronger without any loss of speed. Theismann gave him encouragement in his comeback.

"You have one God-given thing that nobody can give," he told Brown. "You have speed. You have to make people aware of it. You have to make people fear your speed. Then even if you don't use it every time, they still have to defend against it."

Brown was ready. He wanted to become the

other starting receiver opposite Monk.

"I know what it's all about carrying the load," Brown said. "I'm going to go out and try to help as much as possible. With Art on the other side getting double-teamed, I should draw a lot of single coverage. And if I catch a few big passes and start drawing attention, that will take some of the coverage off Art."

At 5'10" Brown was the tallest of a trio of receivers fondly called the "Smurfs." The other two were Virgil Seay, who at 5'8", started and caught 28 passes as a rookie in 1981, and Alvin Garrett, 5"7", who was picked up as a free agent near the end of the season to play on special teams. Both had fine speed although Seay was perhaps a step faster. Like Garrett, Seay was also a free agent, one of the 43 that Gibbs had in training camp. In 1981, Seay played in every game and caught 38 passes averaging 18.2 yards a catch, the best on the team.

Running back Terry Metcalf originated the nickname "Smurfs" after the lovable inch-and-a-half, blue-and-white television characters.

"The limit for being a Smurf is 5'10"," said Garrett. "I'm really 6'5". You just can't see the rest of me. I wasn't too small when I played with the Giants. The reason they let me go was that all their backs got hurt. They had six receivers, so they cut me to pick up a running back."

The running backs that Gibbs was counting on were John Riggins and Joe Washington. Gibbs felt that Riggins needed 1981 to totally come back from his brief retirement the year before. Still, Riggins managed to gain 714 yards which was second only to Washington's 916 yards. It marked the first time in Redskin history that two backs gained over 700 yards. However, Gibbs was a bit concerned about Washington, who was voted the team's most valuable player. The small, but versatile back who also led the team in pass receiving, had had off-season surgery on his knee.

The Redskins' two reserve backs, Wilbur Jackson and Clarence Harmon, were also coming off injuries in 1981. Harmon was sidelined after the fifth game with a separated shoulder, and Jackson sat out the remainder of the season, having reinjured his knee after the sixth game. Since Gibbs planned on switching Metcalf to wide receiver, his only durable back appeared to be Riggins.

The backfield situation placed more pressure on the offensive line. That was also an area of concern in 1981. It was young and inexperienced, the only veteran being ten-year tackle George Starke. At 260 pounds, he was the leanest of the group. It caused line coach Joe Bugel to call the rest of them "Hogs." Bugel, who was brought in from Houston by Gibbs to rebuild the line, stood looking at guard Russ Grimm and center Jeff Bostic one day on the practice field. Laughing to himself, he thought the two actually reminded him of hogs.

"They were short guys with big bellies," said Bugel. "I started to say to the whole line at practice, 'Okay, you hogs, let's go down in the pen and hit those sleds.' Some guys might have resented it, but those guys loved it."

From that day on they were affectionately called "Hogs." Redskin fans fell in love with them. Bugel instilled pride in the unit by giving them white T-shirts trimmed in burgundy and gold with an angry-looking hog in the center. Bugel was given the name Boss Hog. The players were required to wear the Hog shirt at least one day a week. If they failed to do so, they were fined $5. Bugel established a Boss Hog Fund, and the fine money was used at the end of the season for a Hog Feast.

The players took the Hog Club seriously. Not everyone could become a member, and, as a result, it turned into a very exclusive club. It was the sort of pride that Bugel wanted to pull his young line together. There are only ten bona fide Hogs. They are: Bostic; Grimm; guards Mark May, Fred Dean and Ron Saul (who was on injured reserves at the time); tackles Joe Jacoby and Starke; tight ends Rick Walker, Don Warren and Riggins, who was given a T-shirt midway through the 1982 season.

"Our rookie tackle Don Laster wanted to buy a shirt, but we wouldn't sell him one," disclosed Bugel. "This is an exclusive group. You only get in on a majority vote."

Nevertheless, Bugel still had to shape up his Hogs. He did so dramatically by moving players around until they fit. The first thing he did was to cut Melvin Jones, who was a starting guard in 1981. Then he moved May from tackle to replace Jones, despite the fact that May had never played guard before. Bugel had made similar moves in 1981 when he switched Grimm, who was a center, to guard and installed Bostic as the starting center. Grimm responded to the challenge of never playing the position before by being named to the all-NFL Rookie Team. Starke remained at tackle, where he had always played, and Walker became a starter along with Warren when Gibbs went to a two-tight end offense after the fifth week of the 1981 season.

Jacoby was the biggest surprise of all of Bugel's Hogs. Without earning any recognition at the University of Louisville, he was signed as a relatively unknown free agent. When he joined the Redskins, Gibbs mistakenly thought he was a defensive lineman. Gibbs wanted to cut him on the final day of training camp. However, Bugel liked Jacoby's size and persuaded Gibbs to keep him a little longer. The second month of the season Jacoby filled in for the injured May. He has been a starter ever since.

Bugel's line was designed with an emphasis on size. His theory was predicated on a rules' change several years before, allowing offensive linemen more freedom with their hands. Before the change, quick, hard-hitting linemen were the vogue. Bugel quickly reverted to the bigger linemen for blocking purposes, both for the pass and the run. His line averaged 273 pounds, perhaps the heaviest in the NFL. Jacoby was the heaviest at 295, followed by May at 288; Grimm, 273; Starke, 260; and Bostic at 255.

Starke's weight of 260 pounds is considered light for a tackle.

"George was never a very good technical player," revealed Bugel. "He relied on his athletic ability, but now he could play another four years the way he's improved. Jacoby is the most coachable player I've been around. He has great football sense. Grimm makes me bubble all over. He's so sound. He never makes a wrong step. Bostic may become the best center in the league. He's very, very consistent, but he has to be, with all the nose men we face. We call May 'Big Foot' because he has size 16 feet. He isn't pretty out there; he's a slasher who makes up for lack of athletic ability by determination. Fred Dean is our sixth man. He comes off the bench and never misses a step."

Grimm is the leader of the unit. He is a savage performer, reminiscent of the old-time football players who played for the love of the game above all else. Despite his tenaciousness, he is low-key. He shrugs at the thought of making a great deal of money playing pro football, and then later retiring to a high-profile, company-executive job.

"I'm not a 9-to-5 person," says Grimm. "I want to be outside. I'm a construction worker. I want to go to work, eat my lunch, work some more, go to a bar, have a beer, go home and eat. We're blue-collar guys all the way. If we don't play football, we don't have any other job. You have to be a little loose in the head to play offensive line, and you have to be able to play with

Running back Joe Washington kept going all season, playing

pain. Besides, if we don't play well, being a Hog wouldn't be as much fun. And, we always want to have some fun.

"We started meeting at Mark May's house. We'd watch television and chug a few beers, stuff like that. We had some T-shirts made up, but we wanted to keep the Hogs small and private. It was just a way of showing we have a lot of pride as offensive linemen. We're not trying to make a big

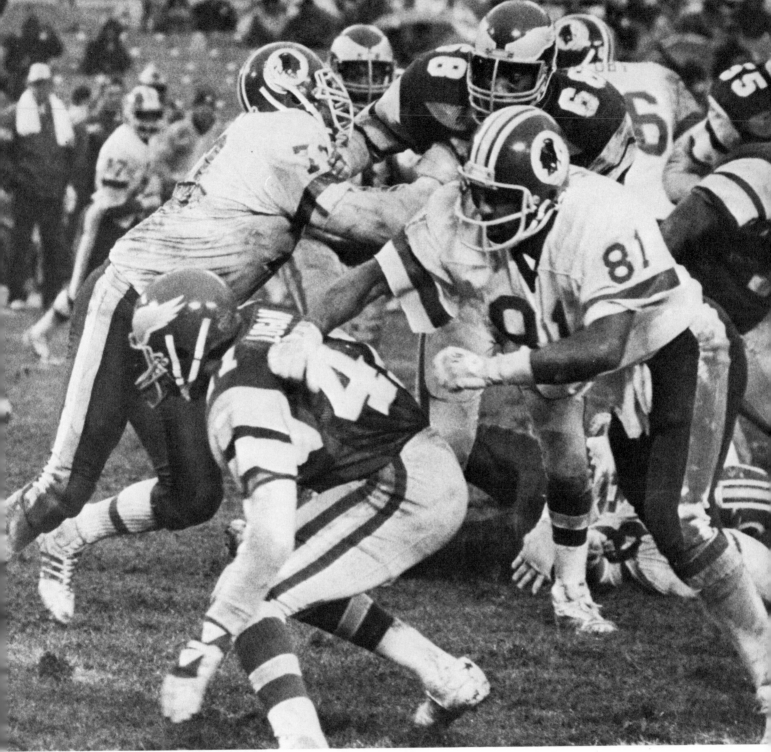

with pain from a knee that required surgery once the campaign ended.

thing out of it. We don't have anything for sale. We're not endorsing anything. We're just proud of our play.''

Jacoby looked back at his rookie season and wondered if he would ever become a Hog, let alone make the team. A Washington scout signed him in the spring of 1981 after he was passed by in the college draft.

"I remember the first time I met coach Gibbs," recalled Jacoby. "After I signed, he told me, 'You have a good opportunity to make the team as a defensive lineman.' I just sat across from him, looking at him, and didn't say a thing. I was just happy to be there. Later that day Gibbs learned of his error. From what I understand, he wasn't very pleased about it. But, there wasn't anything he could do about it."

Bugel's Hogs were indeed coming together.

Kicker Mark Moseley came through with his finest season, booting a record-setting 23 consecutive field goals before his streak was snapped in the final game of the year. His 20 of 21 on the year set an NFL record for percentage, 95.2.

Their selectivity gave them a sense of belonging and accomplishment. Even May didn't mind sharing his guard play with Dean. May excelled at the straight-ahead power block while Dean did his best work on pulling for the running plays and setting up screen passes.

"It's terrific," exclaimed May at the impact the Hogs were making. "No one minds being called a Hog. I mean how many times have offensive linemen gotten this kind of attention?"

No single player appreciated the Hogs more than Riggins. He depended on the Hogs' power blocking to gain yards. "Just wait until this line gets really great," chided Riggins.

Like Grimm, Riggins was a throwback to the football player of the 1930's. He was also well liked by the Hogs even though he achieved more identity than any of the interior linemen.

"Sure, he's the highest paid guy on the team," said Grimm. "But look at him—army boots and camouflage jacket, a typical blue-collar guy like us. He's no speedster. He's not one of those nifty runners. He's from the old school. John says, 'You block for me, I'll get some yards for you.' He's the type of guy who is hard to get close to. He doesn't chatter away. I don't think he lets people get close to him, but he lets you know if you make a good block. He's great to play with."

Riggins was the Hogs' kind of guy, indeed. Bostic realized how important the 1982 season might be to Riggins.

"John's getting into the downhill side of his career," Bostic said in reference to the fact that Riggins was 33 years old. "He's eight to ten years older than most of us. He never made the Super Bowl when he was with the New York Jets. I know he wants one."

Veteran kicker Mark Moseley was also dreaming of a Super Bowl. At 34, the former free agent was beginning his ninth season with Washington. The memory of Jim O'Brien's game-winning kick for Baltimore in Super Bowl V still created excitement for him. He had been hoping to do the same thing before his career was over. Despite years of dependable service, Moseley's chances of remaining with Washington appeared slim. The last two years hadn't been too good. After leading the NFL in field goals with 25 of 33 attempts in 1979, Moseley showed signs of slipping. In 1980 he was 18 of 33 and in 1981, 19 of 30. He also missed seven extra points in two years, causing some suspicions about his leg.

Gibbs was so concerned with Moseley that he had another kicker in camp. Rookie Dan Miller, an eleventh-round draft pick and eleven years younger than Moseley, provided the veteran with his first serious challenge in a number of years. For a good part of the pre-season games, it appeared that Miller would displace Moseley. However, in the final pre-season test against Cincinnati, Miller was errant on two field goal attempts from 45 yards and 37 yards, which cost him his chance to become the team's new kicker. The competition was not lost on Moseley, who appeared to be working harder.

"Probably too much was made of it," Moseley said. "There wasn't much competition at the other positions during camp, so this was something to write about. The kid was a good kicker. I knew Coach Gibbs would make the right decision.

"I'd be lying if I didn't say it really bothered me. I'm only human. When your job is endangered, you fight back."

It wasn't the first time during his career that Moseley was faced with adversity. He was originally drafted by the Philadelphia Eagles in 1970 and cut the following year. He played with Houston for two years and was released a second time. In 1973, at the young age of 25, Moseley was out of football, disillusioned and not knowing what to do. He grabbed a job digging septic tanks, while his wife, Sharon, taught high school. Every day Moseley anxiously waited for his wife to come home. They would drive to a city park in Livingston, Texas, and with his wife acting as the holder, he would practice kicking field goals. That year he wrote letters to almost every team in the NFL, hoping for another chance.

"I never heard a word from any of them," Moseley said. "But early the next year the Redskins signed me as a free agent. I spent two years wondering if I ever would get the chance to kick in the NFL again."

Moseley has been the Redskins' kicker every year since beating out Curt Knight that season. He went on to lead the NFL in field goals in 1976, 1977 and 1979. Over the years, his artful high kicks won many last-minute victories. In a sense, he is a rarity among field goal kickers. Not only does he wear five pair of socks on his kicking foot, but his shoe is square in front. He is one of only two straight-ahead kickers left in the league.

"I think the straight-on kicker has an advantage, especially in bad weather," Moseley points out. "If the field is slippery, I can keep my plant foot under me better, and I can get the ball up faster. I feel I'm at my best when the game is on the line. When George Allen was here, it seemed like every year we had two, three, four games decided by field goals, and that's where I learned to handle pressure. Yet, guys were a lot more uptight under Allen. Every week for seven years it was, 'This is the biggest game of your life.' That was his favorite saying. Everybody was so tight for playoff games that you could hear your shoes squeak as you walked down the hall of the hotel."

Physically, Moseley appeared stronger this summer. In recent years, he had been troubled with nagging muscle pulls in his leg. He switched his training regimen. Instead of working with free weights, he was advised by strength coach Dan Riley to try the Nautilus method during the off season. Moseley never felt better. He felt confident when he reported to training camp.

"Even before camp, I felt this was going to be my best season ever," said Moseley. "I don't know why. I just knew it. My goal was to go a full season without missing a kick. Will any kicker ever do that? I think I'll do it this year. I think I can kick for a lot more years. I've lost maybe a couple of yards, but I still feel confident from a long way out. It will be a matter now of maintaining my strength for as long as possible.

"This club is a lot more relaxed than any I've been on. It's just a great mesh of people. You don't often find a group this large that doesn't have personality conflicts of some kind. There are

never any fights in practice. People are always joking around."

One of the biggest jokers is Mike Nelms, Washington's premier kick returner. While some players imitate animal noises, Nelms derives satisfaction in making bird sounds. Not just ordinary backyard birds, but the shrill sound of jungle birds. Nelms began doing the eerie, high-pitched wild-bird calls after seeing a couple of Tarzan movies several years ago.

"It comes from being a crazy football player," Nelms explained. "Some howl like wolves, some bark like dogs. I do bird calls. I've heard 'em in Tarzan movies. I've heard them in the wilderness. I don't even know what they are, but I've been able to imitate them."

As a kick returner, Nelms doesn't have any imitators. He is acknowledged as the best in the league. The last two years, he received the ultimate recognition by being named to the Pro Bowl. He is the only member of the Redskins to achieve this honor. However, like Moseley, at first he wasn't recognized for his abilities as a football player.

Nelms was drafted by the Buffalo Bills on the seventh round of the 1977 draft. The 6'1" Nelms was a defensive backfield star, and once intercepted three passes in a single game while also high jumping 6'7" for the track team. He lasted until the final cut with Buffalo before being released without any show of interest from other teams. When the Hamilton Tiger-Cats of the Canadian Football League offered him a three-year contract, he took it. After the 1979 season, Nelms wasn't happy with the low salary he was offered. He shopped around the NFL and was signed by Washington as a free agent for the 1980 season.

"It's a blow to your ego when you get cut," Nelms said. "I knew I could play the game, and I hoped that one day I could show the Bills they were in error. So I went to play in Canada. I always considered myself a pro football player and I wanted to eat and pay my bills."

In his first season with Washington, Nelms averaged 21.3 yards on kickoff returns. In 1981 he led the NFL with a 29.7 average, despite playing the first month of the season with a cast to protect a broken thumb. Nelms is also a dangerous punt-return expert who has never signaled for a fair catch in a very hazardous profession. Despite the risk of more frequent injuries, Nelms surprisingly prefers to return punts ahead of kickoffs.

"I've always favored returning punts more than kickoffs," revealed Nelms. "I think it is more conducive to my style. I'm able to move laterally and find holes better. I like the challenge of catching and then returning punts. You really don't have to be able to catch the ball all that well to return kicks. Returning kickoffs is like a war. You have two armies out there, and, as soon as they blow the whistle, they just charge at each other. Emotionally and mentally I prefer punts. It's more difficult to be a good punt-return man. There's more ad libbing to it than kickoffs. Kickoff returns are more basic. All you have to do is have good hands and find the holes. For punt returns you need good hands, speed, ability, coordination, peripheral vision, courage, and, I guess, you need to be a little crazy.

"I love returning kicks. You have to be a little crazy to appreciate it. I appreciate it. I see the art form. It's a challenging, dangerous, exciting job. All eyes are on you. Your moment is brief. You get one shot. You may not get anything on your next return, but you may turn around the game on the one after that. This isn't a job for everyone. Many people just don't like it. You can fumble the ball and foul up the team, and not everyone wants to risk that.

"I have a genuine love for the job, and I don't think fair catches are necessary. I find them boring. If the game was on the line, closing seconds, and we needed field position and couldn't risk a fumble, I might fair catch."

It was something Gibbs thought about, too. He pointed it out to Nelms one day.

"We've talked to Nelms about it," admitted Gibbs. "We've told him there was a time to fair catch. So far he just hasn't seen the time. He's just a gifted guy when it comes to fielding the ball. In practice he does something I've never seen anyone do. Again and again, he'll turn and catch punts behind his back."

Gibbs actually never gave a second thought to whether Nelms would fair catch a punt every once in a while. What occupied his mind was his defense. He felt confident about his offense coming together after Theismann and the others took nearly a full season to learn it. Gibbs spent most of his time thinking about the defense, even to the point of changing from the 4-3 to the 3-4. He experimented with the new alignment during the early weeks of training camp and, in an effort to strengthen the defense, switched Darryl Grant from the offensive line to the defensive unit.

"We just didn't have good enough defensive end play last season either against the run or as pass rushers," Gibbs noted. "If our ends don't come along, then maybe we will have to go the 3-4."

Ever since he was drafted on the first round in 1980, Art Monk has been Washington's big play receiver.

In 1981, both starting ends, Dexter Manley and Mat Mendenhall, were rookies. Manley was drafted on the fifth round, while Mendenhall was a second round pick in the 1980 draft. However, Mendenhall never got to play because of intestinal problems that sidelined him the entire season.

Even in Washington on a unit that doesn't contain any household names, Manley, despite his youth, is the most visible Redskin. At 6'3" and 253 pounds, he is quick for his size. It was his speed on special teams that earned him a starting role at end midway through the season. He acquired additional recognition there with six quarterback sacks. On the basis of what he showed in his first season, Gibbs was depending on Manley for most of the Redskins' pass rush. As a rookie, Manley played with assurance and confidence.

"When you have the problems we did being 0-5, you can point fingers," Manley said about the team's 1981 start. "We didn't. We stuck together as a family and finished 8-8. We got stronger and stronger because of our character. We have more young players than most teams. Maybe we're hungrier than they are. We're not household names, and for us that's good. When I make up my mind, I can just about beat anybody."

Manley grew up in Houston. He feels his big-city upbringing had much to do with his self-assurance. He attended Oklahoma State and for three straight years led the team in tackles for losses, with 39 for 231 yards. In the weight room, he bench pressed over 500 pounds. On Sundays he relaxes riding horses at Coach Jim Stanley's 200-acre farm.

"I'm always making big plays, ever since high school," Manley said. "I remember I did that even when I was a kid playing against big guys. I had drive. I don't just want to play football. I want to make things happen. I always looked up to the best. Julius Erving, Walter Payton, those are my idols. And you know who else I like? Muhammad Ali and Reggie Jackson. God has given me so much ability and has protected me. I don't ever want to be considered mean, just a great football player. Not good, we're all good. I'm not great now, but I'm on my way."

Richie Petitbon, the team's defensive coordinator, thought so, too. "Dexter's a big-play guy," Petitbon said. "He's like a home-run hitter. He's the kind of guy who can win games for you."

With Dave Butz already established at a tackle spot and beginning his seventh year with the Redskins, Gibbs' big pre-season experiment was to try the second year Grant alongside the burly veteran. Grant wasn't big at 6'1", but he weighed a beefy 265 pounds. He was a versatile performer at Rice where he played tackle and center on offense and nose guard and linebacker on defense. Since he wasn't as tall as linemen go, he was generally overlooked in the 1981 draft. However, the Redskins felt fortunate to pick him on the ninth round.

Grant had a frustrating career at Rice. In the four years he played there, the team won only nine games, five of them in his final season. One loss in particular remains fresh in his mind. As a freshman, he stood helplessly on the sidelines in Baton Rouge, Louisiana, as LSU ran up a 77-0 triumph.

"All I remember is those people in the stands yelling, 'We want a hundred, we want a hundred,'" Grant said. "I just stood there and kept thinking, 'I've never been beaten like this. How can you be beaten like this?'"

Gibbs was hoping Grant could make the switch from offense to defense. If he succeeded, he would utilize a four-man front that would have Manley and Mendenhall, who played the run well, at ends and Butz and Grant as tackles. Grant would have to work hard in the months before the season opened to make it happen.

"On this level, it's a difficult thing to do, switch from offense to defense," Grant admitted. "I have to work hard to prove myself."

In the final weeks of the 1981 season the linebacking unit stabilized itself. Neal Olkewicz, who was signed as a free agent in 1979, was firmly established in the middle. At only 6'0", and nicknamed the "Mole" because of his size, Olkewicz was adept at stopping the run. Rich Milot, who was picked on the seventh round of the 1979 draft, had played all three linebacking spots before settling on the right side. He had been hampered with injuries in 1981. He missed five games in all and played while hurt in several others. The team's left-side linebacker, Monte Coleman, also suffered an injury last year. He missed four games early in the season because of a fractured shoulder. Like Milot, Coleman has range and is good on pass coverage. He was drafted on the eleventh round the same year as Milot.

Of all the linebackers, the most seriously injured in 1981 was nine-year veteran Brad Dusek. He had off-season back surgery, suffered a separated shoulder in the final pre-season game and was hurt again before returning to start the final six games. No one knew for certain how much

Running back Clarence Harmon averaged 4.4 yards a run during the 1982 campaign.

The Redskins got good mileage out of tight ends Rick Walker (left) and Don Warren.

Safety Tony Peters (left) and cornerback Jeris White give the Redskins experience in the secondary.

the injuries had taken out of Dusek, 32, or whether he could make the starting unit.

Nevertheless, Washington did have some fine young prospects. One was Mel Kaufman who was signed as a free agent last year. Although he wasn't expected to make the team, Kaufman was impressive in training camp and survived the final cut. He gained some valuable experience replacing Coleman when he was hurt and he did well. The other linebacker the Redskins were looking for help from was Larry Kubin. A sixth round draft choice from Penn State in 1981, Kubin was on injured reserves that year with a damaged knee.

The defensive area that created some doubts was the secondary. Defensive coordinator Richie Petitbon felt that the backs weren't aggressive enough and were what he termed passive. He wanted his backs to become hitters and earn the respect of the opposing team's receivers.

"It was obvious last year that we weren't aggressive enough, especially against the run," Petitbon disclosed. "We have to go after people better. We have to become tougher. You can say all you want about defense, but it still comes down to the fact it has to be played by tough people. I don't like to sit and be passive. I like to attack. The way to win is to force the other guy to lose. If I were a basketball coach, I would press full-court all the time."

The changes that Petitbon was prepared to make were at cornerback. Lemar Parrish, a veteran cornerback, was traded to Buffalo during the off season. The move opened a spot for Jeris White who was starting his third year with the Redskins, having been acquired in a trade from Tampa Bay in 1980. White had a reputation as a hitter.

"You hit those receivers and sometimes you don't have to hit them again because they will run the same pattern and they think, 'Am I going to get hit again?'" White said.

At the other cornerback spot was Joe Lavender, a ten-year veteran. Although he had good size at 6'4", Lavender was 33 years old, and age was becoming a factor. It was the main reason why the Redskins made Vernon Dean their first priority by selecting him on the second round of the 1982 draft. Like White, Dean also had a reputation as a hitter and even though he was a rookie then, he was expected to push Lavender for a starting job.

"I really don't know if receivers are scared or not when you hit them," Dean said. "But the next time they go over the middle, maybe they will look for you to try to tuck the ball a little quicker and drop it instead of catching it."

Washington was set at safeties. Both Tony Peters and Mark Murphy were veterans. Although starting his fourth season with the Redskins, Peters had played his first four years with the Cleveland Browns. Petitbon wanted both players to take more charge on the field instead of waiting for things to happen. He wanted both of them to force the action, come up quicker on the runs and go for the interception on pass plays.

"We have to make sure this year that the receivers know we are out there," Peters said.

Murphy was signed as a free agent out of Colgate in 1977. He led the team in interceptions in 1981 with seven and was the leading tackler for the third straight year after becoming a starter in 1979. At 6'4" and 210 pounds, Murphy was the intimidator of the secondary. He looked at his success as that of an overachiever.

"Put me in a computer and it will reject me," Murphy contends. "I wasn't drafted. I was a free agent when George Allen was coaching here. I was his type of player. I was graduating from Colgate with a B.A. in economics. General Electric offered me a job in financial management in Schenectady, and if the Redskins didn't sign me, I would have gone to work there or in a bank."

As the Redskins prepared for their second season under Gibbs, they appeared as good if not better than the team that won 8 of their 11 games in the 1981 season. Theismann was more confident of Gibbs' offensive philosophy, and the young offensive line had matured after a year of experience. There appeared an abundance of linebackers with only the defensive line and a more aggressive secondary remaining questionable. On paper, the 1982 Redskins appeared stronger.

"I feel better about this team than any other since I've been here," Beathard said. "Sometimes you can't explain why you think something good will happen, but you just believe it. And I believe that about this team."

During the hot summer days at Carlisle little did anyone realize just how good....

Charlie Brown looks over his shoulder to pull down a 78-yard touchdown pass from Joe Theismann in the third quarter.

GAME ONE
PHILADELPHIA

There didn't seem to be any concern that the Redskins lost all four of their pre-season games. Gibbs didn't plan any wholesale changes in personnel for the regular season opener against the Eagles in Philadelphia. The Eagles appeared in Super Bowl XV only two years earlier. Now they were one of the teams the Redskins had to beat to win an Eastern Conference championhsip. A hot, sunny day, with temperature at the 82-degree level, made playing quite uncomfortable.

The first time the Eagles got the ball, they scored. They drove 67 yards in 10 plays when Wilbert Montgomery went four yards up the middle. Tony Franklin added the conversion for a 7-0 Eagle lead. With three minutes left in the period, Franklin added to the margin. He kicked a 44-yard field goal to give Philadelphia a 10-0 edge when the period ended.

With less than 2½ minutes remaining in the first half, Washington finally got on the scoreboard. Theismann hit Monk with a five-yard touchdown pass to culminate an 87-yard march that took 11 plays. Then, just before the half ended, Washington took the lead. They went 46 yards on five plays, Theismann connecting with Brown on an eight-yard touchdown pass. Moseley's extra point gave the Redskins a 14-10 lead. However, Franklin's second 44-yard field goal with only one second left trimmed Washington's edge to 14-13 at halftime.

The Eagles got the lead back when they took the second-half kickoff and rumbled for 86 yards in just eight plays. Montgomery scored from two yards out for his second touchdown of the game. The next time Philadelphia got the ball back, Montgomery scored a third time. Halfway through the quarter, he caught a 42-yard touchdown pass from Ron Jaworski. When the period ended, the Eagles appeared in command with a 27-14 lead.

However, in just one play, Theismann brought the Redskins back. He connected with a 78-yard touchdown pass with Brown with 11 minutes left in the game to draw Washington to within 27-21. He then directed the Redskins on a 48-yard drive in five plays to give Washington the lead once again. Riggins went across from two yards out, and Moseley added the extra point to give the Redskins a 28-27 edge with 6:06 left in the game. Moments later when the Eagles gambled and lost on a fourth down play, Moseley added to Washington's margin. He kicked a 30-yard field goal that sent the Redskins into a 31-27 lead.

But the Eagles came back. Amazingly, they went 90 yards in 15 plays. Jaworski got the Eagles back on top with a four-yard touchdown pass to Harold Carmichael. After Franklin converted, the Redskins looked at a 34-31 deficit with only 58 seconds left on the clock.

Undismayed, Theismann rallied the Redskins. He connected on three straight passes after missing his first to get Washington into Eagle territory. Then he ran for four yards to the Eagle 31 where he called time out with just six seconds remaining to play. Moseley came in to attempt a pressure-packed 48-yard field goal that would tie the game. Only a second remained when Moseley's kick sailed over the crossbars to send the game into overtime, 34-34.

Washington won the coin toss and didn't wait to score. Hitting on all five passes he threw, Theismann led the Redskins to the Eagle nine-yard line. At that point, Moseley sent the Redskins home happy with a 26-yard field goal that gave the Redskins a well earned 37-34 triumph.

"I don't know what we did, I just know we came out on top," Gibbs said. "I'm thoroughly exhausted—like everyone else is."

SEPTEMBER 12, 1982
AT VETERANS STADIUM,
PHILADELPHIA

Washington	0	14	0	20	3	— 37
Philadelphia	10	3	14	7	0	— 34

P—Montgomery 4 run (Franklin kick)
P—FG, Franklin, 44
W—Monk, 5 pass from Theismann
    (Moseley kick)
W—Brown, 8 pass from Theismann
    (Moseley kick)
P—FG, Franklin, 44
P—Montgomery 2 run (Franklin kick)
P—Montgomery, 42 pass from Jaworski
    (Franklin kick)
W—Brown, 78 pass from Theismann
    (Moseley kick)
W—Riggins 2 run (Moseley kick)
W—FG, Moseley, 30
P—Carmichael, 4 pass from Jaworski
    (Franklin kick)
W—FG, Moseley, 48
W—FG, Moseley, 26

GAME TWO
TAMPA BAY

More hot weather faced the Redskins in the wake of their second consecutive road game. Only this time it was worse. The 90-degree weather in Tampa Bay was hotter than in Philadelphia, and by the time the teams were ready for the kickoff, a driving rain made playing conditions more deplorable.

The Buccaneers were regarded as a dark horse in the Central Division of the NFC. Although they had dropped their opening game to Minnesota 17-10, the Bucs had a strong defensive team led by All-Pro linebacker Lee Roy Selmon. With the sloppy playing conditions, no team could afford to make any mistakes and still hope to win. Despite inclement weather, a crowd of 66,187 turned out in open Tampa Stadium.

Washington scored first. The third time the Redskins got the ball, Theismann took them 60 yards in ten plays. After running Riggins on five of six plays, he caught the Bucs off guard with a two-yard touchdown pass to Brown. Unfortunately, Moseley missed the extra point and Washington's lead remained at 6-0. However, the next time the Redskins got the ball, Moseley added to the lead. He kicked a 35-yard field goal to put Washington ahead 9-0 as the first period ended.

On the first play of the second quarter, quarterback Doug Williams got the Buccaneers right back into the game. He brought the crowd to their feet under their umbrellas by connecting on a 62-yard touchdown pass with wide receiver Kevin House. Bill Capece never got his kick off because of a bad snap, and Washington's lead remained at 9-6.

Both teams had trouble moving the ball after that. The Redskins got the next opportunity to score when linebacker Neal Olkewicz recovered Williams' fumble on the Tampa Bay 10-yard line. After Riggins got to the two-yard line on two carries, Theismann missed on a third down pass. Moseley came on, however, and booted a 21-yard field goal which gave Washington a 12-6 lead.

The Redskins' special teams provided the team's next score. On the following series, the Bucs couldn't move, and Larry Swider was back on his 10-yard line waiting to punt. Cornerback Curtis Jordan broke through and blocked Swider's punt. The ball landed in the end zone where Jordan fell on it for a touchdown. Moseley missed the extra point and when the half ended five minutes later, the Redskins had a wet 18-6 lead.

It remained that way when the third period came to a close. Neither team ever threatened to score on the soggy field, although it had stopped raining. The heavy footing slowed both teams, and the Redskins managed only two first downs on the two offensive series they had.

Early in the fourth period, Tampa Bay scored. Passing under heavy pressure from the Washington defense, Williams, nevertheless, led the Buccaneers 54 yards on seven plays with James Wilder running the final seven for the touchdown. Capece's conversion trimmed Washington's margin to 18-13.

The Redskins came back. They took the kickoff and went 63 yards in 16 plays and got as far as the Tampa Bay two-yard line. Moseley came through with a 19-yard field goal that stretched Washington's lead to 21-13. It stayed that way until the game ended four minutes later.

Riggins carried 34 times in the game for 136 yards, the eighteenth 100-yard game of his career. The 34 rushing attempts tied a team record established 45 years earlier by Cliff Battles.

What the Redskins and the other teams feared now was a players' strike. No one knew how long it would last....

**SEPTEMBER 19, 1982
AT TAMPA STADIUM,
TAMPA**

Washington	9	9	0	3	—	21
Tampa Bay	0	6	0	7	—	13

W—Brown, 8 pass from Theismann (kick failed)
W—FG, Moseley, 35
TB—House, 62 pass from Williams (kick failed)
W—FG, Moseley, 21
W—Jordan recovered blocked punt in end zone (kick failed)
TB—Wilder 7 run (Capece kick)
W—FG, Moseley, 19

Defensive end Dexter Manley tried to run for a touchdown with a recovered fumble in rain-soaked Tampa Stadium.

Wide receiver Virgil Seay grabs Joe Theismann's pass before stepping out of bounds.

GAME THREE
NEW YORK GIANTS

Following the unprecedented eight-week players' strike, nobody, least of all Gibbs, knew what to expect when the Redskins and the 27 other NFL teams returned to continue the season. Theismann had kept the team together by holding workouts three days a week in a small public park in Reston, Virginia. As luck would have it, Washington was on the road again for the third straight time. Since three of the four pre-season games were also out of town, loyal Redskin rooters hardly had a chance to know their own players.

The Giants had dropped their two opening games, but they couldn't be taken lightly. Like Philadelphia and Tampa Bay, the Giants had also appeared in the playoffs the year before. A strong defense had made them tough. In addition, after such a long strike, it was like starting the season all over again. Only this time no one could determine what shape the players were in. Gibbs was hoping the Redskins could regain the momentum they had demonstrated before the ill-fated strike.

He felt good after the opening kickoff. The Redskins drove 73 yards in 12 plays to score first. Theismann flipped a quick one-yard pass to Otis Wonsley for the touchdown. Moseley added the extra point, and Washington moved into a 7-0 lead. The period ended when the Giants' only attempt at getting on the scoreboard failed as Joe Danelo's 49-yard field-goal try sailed wide to the right.

Theismann didn't show any adverse effects of the strike in the early moments of the second period. After he scrambled for 11 yards on the last play of the first quarter, he hooked up with Brown on a 39-yard touchdown pass on the third play of the period. When Moseley supplied the extra point, the Redskins led 14-0.

The irrepressible Manley positioned Washington's next touchdown a minute later. He intercepted Scott Brunner's pass on the Giant 18-yard line to give the Redskins a golden opportunity. They didn't waste it either. Four plays later, on first down, Riggins drove in from the two-yard line. Moseley accounted for the conversion and Washington swept to a 21-0 lead with 11 minutes remaining in the half.

Following the kickoff, New York finally made some points. They had to settle for Danelo's 20-yard field goal when their 67-yard march stalled on the two-yard line. When the half ended, the Redskins appeared in control.

However, early in the third period, the Giants forced a turnover. Linebacker Frank Marion blocked Jeff Hayes' punt at midfield, and the Giants recovered the ball on the Redskin 26-yard line. Two plays later, Brunner raised Giant fans' hopes with a 26-yard touchdown pass to wide receiver Johnny Perkins. Danelo's point after touchdown reduced Washington's margin to 21-10.

Theismann was unruffled. In a ball-control drive that consumed 8:48, he got the Redskins down as far as the Giants' 20-yard line. It was close enough for Moseley to kick a 37-yard field goal that gave the Redskins a 24-10 lead when the period closed.

Still, the Giants came back. They drove 77 yards in ten plays to keep close to the Redskins. Cliff Chatman dove over for the touchdown from a yard out. Danelo tacked on the extra point, and the Giants were only a touchdown away, 24-17, with 12 minutes to play.

That was as close as they got. Near the game's end, Theismann set up the Redskins' final score with a third down 37-yard pass completion to Virgil Seay on the Giants' 20-yard line. After Riggins carried three times to the 12, Moseley booted a 29-yard field goal with 1:23 remaining to finish off the Giants, 27-17.

"Hell, I spent all eight weeks keeping the guys together," Theismann said. "I'd have been pretty disappointed if we didn't look effective."

NOVEMBER 21, 1982
AT GIANTS STADIUM,
EAST RUTHERFORD, N.J.

Washington	7	14	3	3	— 27
NY Giants	0	3	7	7	— 17

W—Wonsley, 1 pass from Theismann (Moseley kick)
W—Brown, 39 pass from Theismann (Moseley kick)
W—Riggins 2 run (Moseley kick)
NY—FG, Danelo, 20
NY—Perkins, 26 pass from Brunner (Danelo kick)
W—FG, Moseley, 37
NY—Chatman 1 run (Danelo kick)
W—FG, Moseley, 29

GAME FOUR
PHILADELPHIA

It was a cold, wet afternoon on November 28 when Washington fans finally got their first opportunity to see the Redskins play at home. It must have felt like an eternity. Normally, the football season is winding down at Thanksgiving time. However, in anticipation of the playoffs in an abbreviated season, it was just heating up for the Redskins.

They were unbeaten, having won all three of their road games. Since the regular season would only include 9 games instead of the normal 16, figure filberts concluded if Washington won five games, they would make the playoffs. Although this was only their fourth game, the Redskins were facing the Eagles for the second time. Even after losing a close 18-14 game to the AFC champion Cincinnati Bengals the previous week, Philadelphia at 1-2 was also thinking of the playoffs. The game was very important to them.

Washington was on the move after taking the opening kickoff until cornerback Roynell Young intercepted a Theismann pass on the Eagle 10-yard line. However, when the Redskins got the ball back, Moseley gave them a 3-0 lead with a 45-yard field goal, a lead they carried into the second period.

Five minutes into the quarter, Theismann had the crowd cheering. He collaborated with Brown on a 65-yard touchdown play that stunned the Eagles. Moseley's conversion gave the Redskins a 10-0 lead. The end of the first half saw the Washington defense in control of the Eagles.

In the third quarter, the Eagles struck swiftly. After five minutes had gone by, they got a 41-yard field goal from Tony Franklin to cut Washington's lead to 10-3. Then the next time they got the ball, they came dangerously close to tying the game. They scored a touchdown when Ron Jaworski tossed a 44-yard touchdown pass to big Harold Carmichael. However, with a chance to deadlock the contest, Franklin missed the extra point as the Redskins clung to a tenuous 10-9 edge.

The Redskins needed a big play to regain the momentum and they got it on the kickoff. Mike Nelms returned Franklin's kickoff 58 yards to provide the Redskins with excellent field position. After Theismann was sacked for a 13-yard loss, he got the Redskins close enough on a third down pass completion for Moseley to line up a 43-yard field goal attempt. Moseley delivered to give Washington a bit more breathing room, 13-9, when the third period reached an end.

It remained for the Washington defense to preserve the thin lead and they did. First, Mark Murphy thwarted Jaworski by stopping an Eagle advance with an interception on the Redskin 15-yard line. Then, when the Eagles were mounting one final drive, Tony Peters picked off a Jaworski pass with 1:43 left in the game. Riggins ran the clock out at that point to give the Redskins a tough, 13-9 victory.

"Our defense and our special teams held us up today," Theismann said in the wake of suffering his first two interceptions of the season after 98 passing attempts. "The most important statistic I worry about is wins and losses. Right now we're rolling, and I want to keep us rolling."

It was the third straight time that the Eagles had lost to the Redskins, and their chances for the playoffs had dropped considerably. Philadelphia coach Dick Vermeil was impressed with the Redskins.

"They're a darn good football team," he said.

NOVEMBER 29, 1982
AT RFK STADIUM,
WASHINGTON, D.C.

Washington	3	7	3	0	— 13
Philadelphia	0	0	9	0	— 9

W—FG, Moseley, 45
W—Brown, 65 pass from Theismann (Moseley kick)
P—FG, Franklin, 41
P—Carmichael, 44 pass from Jaworski (kick failed)
W—FG, Moseley, 43

Free safety Mark Murphy breaks up a pass intended for Philadelphia's John Spagnola.

GAME FIVE
DALLAS

No one in Washington needed to be reminded about the Dallas Cowboys. For a number of years they had been, and still are, the Redskins' fiercest rivals. It was a rivalry that was manifested in the years when George Allen was coach, and it has intensified to alarming proportions ever since. There is no more important game in the Washington season than the one with the Cowboys.

"It's going to be a big day for our town," Gibbs exclaimed.

Big indeed. Washington was the only team in the entire NFL that was undefeated after four games. Lest anyone forget, long before the strike, the Cowboys were beaten on the first Monday Night game of the season by the Pittsburgh Steelers. Since then, they had won three games in a row and with a 3-1 record were only one game behind the surprising Redskins. Nobody in Dallas had to point out to the Cowboys that a loss to Washington on this first Sunday in December would drop them two games behind in the National Football Conference race, which almost everyone picked them to win.

Besides being possessed with tying Washington for first place, the Cowboys had another incentive. Not that any incentive was needed when Dallas and Washington met, but Dallas coach Tom Landry was seeking his 200th coaching victory, and what better moment to achieve it than against the Redskins. All the drama was there on the field before 54,633 Redskin rooters. It was also perfect football weather—partly sunny and 66 degrees at kickoff.

Neither team could generate much of an offense in the first period which ended scoreless. However, before five minutes had elapsed in the second quarter, the Cowboys scored. Completing a drive that began near the end of the first period, the Cowboys rode 76 yards in ten plays. The payoff was an eight-yard touchdown pass from quarterback Danny White to running back Ron Springs. Rafael Septien made it 7-0 with a perfect placement. At the time, nobody realized it, but that was the extent of scoring in the first half.

Septien extended Dallas' edge to 10-0 when he booted a 31-yard field goal in the opening minutes of the third quarter to put the finishing touches on a 52-yard drive that covered 11 plays. Washington's offense had a difficult time getting untracked. Their task became even greater when Timmy Newsome broke loose on an 18-yard run for a touchdown in the closing five minutes of the period. Septien added the extra point that gave Dallas a 17-0 advantage when the fourth quarter began.

In the beginning of the fourth quarter, Washington's offense began to stir. They penetrated far enough into Dallas' territory for Moseley to attempt a 38-yard field goal on the second play of the final period. Moseley got the Redskins on the scoreboard by connecting on his 14th straight field goal. It gave the Redskins a spark. On the next offensive series, Washington produced its first touchdown. It came when there were ten minutes left in the game as Theismann, who had been sacked seven times, threw a 17-yard touchdown pass to Brown. Moseley's extra point left the Redskins a touchdown away at 17-10.

Washington fans had visions of a tie at that point. However, with about two minutes left in the game, their hopes were dashed. Ron Springs did it on just one play. He shook loose on a 46-yard touchdown run that clinched the victory for Dallas. Septien's extra point finished off the Redskins, 24-10.

"That run really hurt. It was a tight game at that point, and I thought it was our first chance to even it up," Gibbs said.

**DECEMBER 5, 1982
AT RFK STADIUM,
WASHINGTON, D.C.**

Dallas	0	7	10	7	— 24
Washington	0	0	0	10	— 10

D—Springs, 8 pass from White (Septien kick)
D—FG, Septien, 31
D—Newsome 18 run (Septien kick)
W—FG, Moseley, 38
W—Brown, 17 pass from Theismann
   (Moseley kick)
D—Springs, 46 run (Septien kick)

The Redskin defense braces to shut down a Dallas run with linebacker Mel Kaufman searching out the ball carrier.

GAME SIX
ST. LOUIS

After an emotional loss to Dallas, Gibbs had to be wary of a complete team letdown as the Redskins packed for another road game against St. Louis. Washington's first loss of the season, which snapped a seven-game winning streak extending back to the 1981 season, left them with a 4-1 record and a three-way tie with Dallas and Green Bay for the NFC lead.

There was a bit of nostalgia for Gibbs in St. Louis. For five years, he had been an assistant coach of the Cardinals under Don Coryell. The Cardinals, and quarterback Jim Hart, in particular, prospered under the coaching of Gibbs, who functioned as offensive coordinator. Now, however, St. Louis was in a state of transition with Neil Lomax replacing Hart, leading the pesky Cardinals to a 3-2 record with some serious thoughts of the playoffs. A victory over the Redskins would fortify their chances immensely.

On a clear, cold day, the Redskins received the opening kickoff. They couldn't do anything and quickly had to punt. Then Ottis Anderson stunned the Redskin defense on the very first play. Starting on the 10-yard line, Anderson swept around left end and raced for 64 yards before Vernon Dean saved a touchdown by bringing the big fullback down from behind on the Washington 26. It all went for nothing, however, as the Cardinals stalled, and Neal O'Donoghue missed a 26-yard field goal attempt.

On the next series, Washington kept the ball for almost nine minutes. They went 65 yards in 16 plays and scored first when Moseley kicked a 32-yard field goal. The quarter ended two minutes later with Washington in front, 3-0.

A short Cardinal punt gave the Redskins an opportunity to build their lead midway through the second period. Despite two penalties, Washington drove close enough for Moseley to boot a 30-yard field goal that increased their lead to 6-0 at the end of the first half. Although the Cardinals had outgained the Redskins, Washington's defense kept them in check by recovering two fumbles and sacking Lomax twice.

St. Louis was driving with the second half kick-off when once again the alert Washington defense recovered a fumble. Running back Wayne Morris lost the ball on the Redskin 29 and linebacker Neal Olkewicz recovered it. Theismann then directed the Redskins all the way to the Cardinal three-yard line, the big play coming on a 38-yard pass completion to Brown. However, the Redskins couldn't get a touchdown and had to settle for Moseley's 20-yard field goal that stretched Washington's advantage to 9-0.

Within five minutes of the final period, Moseley again made his appearance. After Washington went 65 yards in 15 plays, Moseley came on to kick his fourth field goal from the 24-yard line to give the Redskins a 12-0 lead. Following the kick-off, Hart entered the game for the first time and directed the Cardinals on a 63-yard drive in just ten plays. He produced the game's first touchdown on a five-yard pass to Greg LaFleur. O'Donoghue added the conversion and St. Louis trailed by only five points, 12-7. Hart had one more chance to pull the game out, but missed on his final two pass attempts from the Washington 26-yard line. Moseley was the difference on a slick field.

"Mark kicks well under all conditions," Gibbs said. "He's great on grass, great on turf. Fine in cold weather, fine on ice. We played Philadelphia in mud and he was great. Mark is like steel. He just pounds them through. We can't dominate anybody. It always seems to come down to field goals. I would like to get some more points, but we tried everything in our game plan."

DECEMBER 12, 1982
AT BUSCH STADIUM,
ST. LOUIS, MO.

Washington	3	3	3	3	— 12
St. Louis	0	0	0	7	— 7

W—FG, Moseley, 32
W—FG, Moseley, 30
W—FG, Moseley, 20
W—FG, Moseley, 24
SL—LaFleur, 5 pass from Hart
    (O'Donoghue kick)

Clarence Harmon grabs a short pass from Joe Theismann in the middle of the St. Louis defense.

GAME SEVEN
NEW YORK GIANTS

Since the Green Bay Packers had lost to Detroit the past week, Washington and Dallas remained at the top of the NFC standings with identical 5-1 records. Because the Redskins wouldn't be meeting the Cowboys again in the regular season, they had to make every game count in the final weeks of action prior to the playoffs.

This time they faced another challenge. In meeting the Giants for the second time, Washington was playing a team that was hot. New York had won three games in a row and had evened its record at 3-3. What's more, the Giants now had serious playoff aspirations and realized that a win over the Redskins would almost get them there.

The season was coming down to numbers. The five victories produced by the Redskins assured them of a spot in the playoffs. If they could defeat the Giants, it would assure them of playing at least one game of the playoffs in RFK Stadium. They made the attempt on a snowy day on a wet and soggy field.

Washington appeared on the move with the opening kickoff until Theismann was intercepted by linebacker Brian Kelley on the Giants' 34-yard line. Quarterback Scott Brunner used the turnover to produce the Giants' first touchdown. It came on a 28-yard pass to wide receiver Johnny Perkins. Joe Danelo kicked the extra point, and New York jumped into a 7-0 lead. Driving again, the next time they got the ball, the Redskins were stopped by another turnover. After catching a 25-yard pass from Theismann, Art Monk fumbled on the Giants' 10-yard line.

The Redskins were working on another drive when play resumed in the second period. However, when they stalled after reaching the Giants' three-yard line, Moseley got Washington their first points by booting a 20-yard field goal. Yet turnovers continued to plague the Redskins. As the first half was winding down, cornerback Terry Jackson intercepted Theismann deep in Washington's end of the field. Five plays later, Butch Woolfolk scored a yard out just before the half ended. Danelo's conversion gave the Giants a 14-3 halftime edge simply because the Redskins committed five turnovers which included four Theismann interceptions. It wiped out the large statistical edge the Redskins had at the time.

Following the second-half kickoff, Washington stopped the Giants and scored their first touchdown. Theismann directed the Redskins 80 yards in just ten plays and threw a key block for a touchdown. It came on Joe Washington's 22-yard run midway through the period when he reversed his field on a pass-option play. However, when the reliable Moseley missed his extra point attempt, the score remained 14-9.

Nevertheless, Moseley provided the dramatics in the fourth period. The first time came with 8:23 remaining to play. Putting the Redskins just a field goal away, he tied an NFL record of 20 consecutive field goals when he booted a 31-yarder that narrowed New York's lead 14-12. Yet, he saved the most exciting moment for last. There were only four seconds left on the clock when Moseley lined up a 42-yard field goal attempt. If he made it, he would set an NFL record of 21 consecutive field goals, breaking the mark held by Miami's Garo Yepremian. More important, a successful kick would give the Redskins a 15-14 triumph. Disregarding the pressure, Moseley's kick gracefully sailed over the crossbars as Redskin fans roared.

"It's just a game," Moseley said. "I don't think about pressure. I've got a job to do, just like the quarterback, wide receiver and linebacker."

**DECEMBER 19, 1982
AT RFK STADIUM,
WASHINGTON, D.C.**

NY Giants	7	7	0	0	— 14
Washington	0	3	6	6	— 15

NY—Perkins, 28 pass from Brunner
    (Danelo kick)
W—FG, Moseley, 20
NY—Woolfolk 1 run (Danelo kick)
W—Washington 22 run (kick failed)
W—FG, Moseley, 31
W—FG, Moseley, 42

*Linebacker Rich Milot strips the ball from the arms
of Giant quarterback Scott Brunner.*

GAME EIGHT
NEW ORLEANS

The dramatic win over the Giants clinched a playoff spot for the Redskins for the first time in six years. They were still tied with Dallas at 6-1 after having put a decisive dent in the playoff hopes of both the Giants and the Cardinals.

"Walking off the field after the Giant game you can tell we had broken their hearts," Theismann said. "They really wanted the game. And so did the Cardinals the previous week."

There was quite a bit of playoff analyzing taking place among the players. It was healthy, too, since it would prevent any big letdown following such an emotional win against the Giants. Gibbs welcomed it since the Redskins were heading for New Orleans to face the Saints who would be without quarterback Ken Stabler and leading rusher George Rogers, both of whom were sidelined with injuries.

Washington's thinking now was to win its remaining two games with the hope that maybe some other team, Philadelphia or Minnesota, would upset Dallas. This possibility would allow the Redskins to have a home-field advantage for all three playoff games. The thought was stimulating indeed.

The Redskins didn't wait long to put their thought process to work. The first time they got the ball against the Saints, they scored. Theismann teamed with Brown on a 57-yard touchdown pass. Moseley added the point after to give Washington a 7-0 lead. Actually, that was the extent of the Redskins' offense in the first quarter as they failed to get a first down the next three times they had the ball.

New Orleans tied the game two minutes into the second period. Jimmy Rogers culminated a 58-yard drive that took nine plays by scoring from the four-yard line. Morten Andersen accounted for the extra point that made the score 7-7.

Still, the Redskin offense appeared listless. It finally came to life with less than three minutes remaining in the half. Again, it was a big play that did it. This time Theismann and Brown hooked up on a 58-yard touchdown pass that broke the tie. Moseley's kick gave Washington a 14-7 lead. Just before the half ended, Moseley added to it. A Theismann to Monk pass completion of 36 yards gave Moseley an opportunity to extend his field goal record. He made it 22 in a row with a 36-yard kick that gave the Redskins a 17-7 halftime edge.

Again the Washington offense had trouble moving when the third period got under way. It enabled the Saints to cut the Redskins' lead to a touchdown when Andersen came through with a 36-yard field goal. When the period came to a close, Washington had produced only one of eight third down conversions and had the ball eight minutes less than the Saints.

With nine minutes left in the contest, Moseley stretched his record to 23. He delivered a 45-yard field goal that provided the Redskins with a 20-10 lead. The next time Washington had possession, they scored a touchdown. Joe Washington lit the spark with a 40-yard run. Riggins put the finishing touches on the 63-yard drive by banging across from the one-yard line. Moseley's conversion sealed the win, 27-10.

"We go into every game not with the idea of making one or two big plays, but making seven or eight," Theismann said. "We figure, if they blitz us ten times and we can burn 'em twice, we're doing the job. We feel if they press us, we like to take a shot. We anticipated a blitz on our first two touchdowns, and the Saints gave us what we expected."

DECEMBER 26, 1982
AT THE LOUISIANA SUPERDOME,
NEW ORLEANS, LA.

Washington	7	10	0	10	— 27
New Orleans	0	7	3	0	— 10

W—Brown, 57 pass from Theismann
  (Moseley kick)
NO—J. Rogers 4 run (Anderson kick)
W—Brown, 58 pass from Theismann
  (Moseley kick)
W—FG, Moseley, 36
NO—FG, Anderson, 36
W—FG, Moseley, 45
W—Riggins 1 run (Moseley kick)

Joe Washington tries to spin away from New Orleans cornerback Johnny Poe.

GAME NINE
ST. LOUIS

The playoff puzzle was taking shape. Washington stood alone on top of the NFC standings with a 7-1 record. Dallas had slipped to 6-2 after being upset by Philadelphia, 24-20. It brought joy to Gibbs and his players.

"It's a great feeling to be on top of the conference," Gibbs said. "Now we have a chance to get the home-field advantage if we win this week."

Washington's task was to defeat the St. Louis Cardinals for the second time in a month. The Cardinals were heading for the playoffs with a 5-3 record. Yet, the importance of winning the final regular game of the season pointed to the Redskins. A victory by Washington would enable them to maintain a home-field advantage throughout the remainder of the championship playoffs up to the conference championship game. That was high stakes indeed.

The Cowboys were looking on with great interest. They were in Minnesota for a Monday Night game with the Vikings. If the Redskins lost to the Cardinals, and they, in turn, beat the Vikings, they would gain the home-field advantage since they had already beaten Washington. Washington didn't need any more incentive than that.

The Redskins had to win without the help of Riggins who was sidelined with an injured leg. They also couldn't count on Mike Nelms, their gifted kick-return specialist. They also suffered a severe setback early in the game when Monk went down with a bone fracture in his right foot. It wasn't long after that the Redskins learned that Monk was through for the season.

Theismann and the Washington defense took charge in the face of such adversity. The Washington quarterback opened the scoring, hitting tight end Rick Walker with a 25-yard pass for Walker's first touchdown of the season. Moseley added the conversion and Washington moved into a 7-0 lead. In the second period Theismann struck again. This time he flipped a quick two-yard pass to his other tight end, Clint Didier, who

also scored his first touchdown of the year. Moseley converted and at intermission Washington led, 14-0. Meanwhile, the Redskin defense contained the Cardinals. St. Louis only produced one first down and 18 total net yardage.

Oddly, it turned out to be a game of first achievements or in Moseley's case, disappointment. Clarence Harmon accounted for his first touchdown of the campaign by scoring from a yard out in the third quarter. Moseley's extra point stretched Washington's advantage to 21-0. However, Moseley's record of 23 consecutive field goals came to an end when he missed a 40-yard attempt.

Theismann relied on his arm to get the Redskins their last touchdown in the final period. He threw an eight-yard touchdown pass to Joe Washington to put the game completely out of reach. Moseley closed out the scoring with his conversion, 28-0. It was a total victory, offensively and defensively.

"We're the Rodney Dangerfields of the National Football League," Theismann exclaimed. "All you ever hear about is the Dallas Cowboys. But now that we are 8-1, people had better start taking another look at us."

Moseley didn't look too bad on his missed field goal which snapped his streak.

"Certainly I didn't want to miss, but you begin to wonder just how far you are going to go with the streak," he reasoned. "Now I'll just have to start a new record for the playoffs." ●

JANUARY 2, 1983
AT RFK STADIUM,
WASHINGTON, D.C.

Washington	7	7	7	7	— 28
St. Louis	0	0	0	0	— 0

W—Walker, 25 pass from Theismann (Moseley kick)
W—Didier, 2 pass from Theismann (Moseley kick)
W—Harmon 1 run (Moseley kick)
W—Washington, 8 pass from Theismann (Moseley kick)

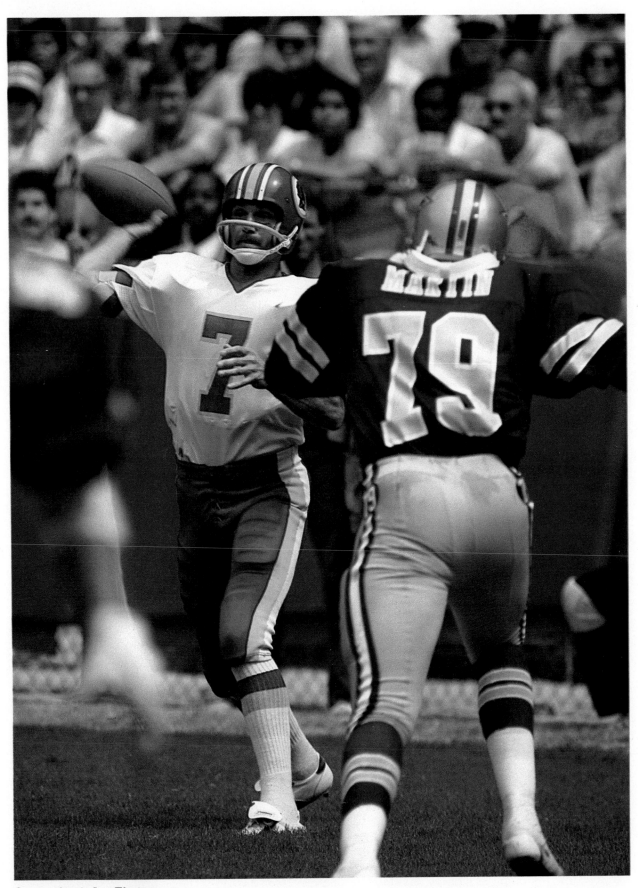

Quarterback Joe Theismann

icker Mark Moseley

Running back John Riggins takes on the Dolphins in Super Bowl XVII.

Love them Hogs.

The offense celebrates a touchdown in Super Bowl XVII.

The Hogs do their thing.

Wide receiver Art Monk

Wide receiver Alvin Garret

Wide receiver Charlie Brown

Kick return specialist Mike Nelms

Defensive end Dexter Manley rises from a conquest.

Defensive tackle Dave Bu

Safety Mark Murphy

Joe Theismann drops back to pass as tackle George Starke offers him protection.

DETROIT PLAYOFF 9
"I Don't Think They Have That Fear Of Us"

It didn't matter that Washington finished 8-1, the best record in the NFC, equaled only by the Los Angeles Raiders in the AFC. It also didn't matter that they still didn't elicit any more respect around the league because of it. What mattered at this point was that the Redskins were in the playoffs for the first time in six years with a group of players, most of whom were free agents and perhaps best described as over-achievers. If Washington's fine record still didn't earn them respect, it did at least reward them with the home-field advantage throughout the playoffs and the NFC championship game. Still the Redskins had to play the games one at a time before reaching the championship. Their first obstacle was the Detroit Lions, an enigmatic team that finished the season with a 4-5 record.

Even Gibbs recognized that despite his club's success, it still hadn't done much to improve its image as a solid football team that was a legitimate Super Bowl contender.

"I think teams fear people like San Diego and Cincinnati, but, being honest, I don't think they have that fear of us," Gibbs admitted. "They are still looking at this team and saying, 'How in the world did these guys get to where they are?' I just don't think they picture us as being one of the teams with the best record. And I don't think anyone will pick us to go the route and win the Super Bowl from now on."

Gibbs' assessment of why his club didn't command the respect most 8-1 teams did, was, to some degree, prompted by a remark made by Detroit coach Monte Clark earlier in the week. Clark had been far from controversial throughout his coaching career but he certainly tweaked the beards of the Washington players with his out-of-character comment.

"The Redskins are sound, solid and they play together well," Clark said. "But I don't think they are a great team. If we were a little healthier, I think we'd match up well."

It took a lot of courage for Clark to make such an inflammatory statement considering the Lions were one of two teams in the playoffs with a losing record. Besides, he had troubles of his own. Because of the Lions' lackluster performance, Clark's job was rumored to be in jeopardy. He also had had trouble throughout most of the season deciding whether Gary Danielson or Eric Hipple should be the team's starting quarterback. The latter, who is more mobile than Danielson, started the first two games of the season. However, it took a relief effort by Danielson to win both contests. After Danielson started

Lions' Dave Pureifory (75) and William Gay (79) jolt ball loose from Joe Theismann.

the next five games, Clark changed back to Hipple who pulled out the playoff, clinching victory over Green Bay in the last game of the season.

"I'm starting Hipple against Washington on a gut decision," Clark said.

Clark also had some injuries to worry about. The most damaging to the Lions' chances being a cartilage injury to the knee of wide receiver Fred Scott. Scott had 156 yards in receptions against the Redskins the previous year in a game Washington won 33-31. Detroit had some key defensive injuries too. Al "Bubba" Baker, Detroit's leading sacker with 8½, had knee and ankle ailments that were expected to limit his playing time. The other injured Lion, middle linebacker Ken Fanetti, would have to play with a heavily taped shoulder to protect a painful separation.

The Redskins weren't without a hospital list either. Monk was definitely out for the playoffs and the Super Bowl. Clarence Harmon was ailing with a strained knee and a cracked wrist bone. Cornerback Vernon Dean had to play with a cast protecting his fractured wrist and wide receiver Virgil Seay, kick returner Mike Nelms and running backs John Riggins and Joe Washington were nursing leg injuries. It was enough to make Gibbs moan.

"I wonder who's going to be lining up when we're all through," Gibbs said. "Our team has overcome everything else. It's just something we'll have to cope with."

Somehow the Redskins managed. No team raised eyebrows around the NFL as much as Washington when they entered the playoffs less than two years after a horrifying 0-5 beginning in 1981. None of the NFL purists could name a superstar or a number one draft choice on the Redskins. Perhaps they could best be described as a blue-collar team that worked hard with an offensive line called the Hogs and a group of diminutive wide receivers known as the Smurfs, who were led by Theismann and Riggins and directed by Gibbs.

"When I think of the Redskins, I think really of just three people," said George Young, general manager of the New York Giants who lost twice to Washington during the 1982 season. "I think of Joe Theismann, Mark Moseley and John Riggins."

It all starts with Theismann. If he is consistent in his play, it transmits itself to the rest of the squad. From a standpoint of consistency alone, Theismann had his best season. At one stage of the campaign, he threw 96 straight passes with-

John Riggins runs into a den of Lions.

out an interception. That, in itself, established the Redskins as a team that never beat itself with turnovers. Theismann's effectiveness was needed game in and game out since Washington had no established superstars to turn to, only dependable key contributors like Moseley and Riggins. Theismann was looked upon as the straw that stirred the drink, and now the Redskins were looking for the champagne that came with post-season victories.

"I've never enjoyed playing more," Theismann said. "We've just begun to tap what this offense can do, which is the real excitement. I feel comfortable with the coaches, with my teammates and myself. I have a good idea of what they want me to do, where I should throw the ball. I no longer feel I have to make things happen for us to win. If I just do my job right, things will happen by design.

"The one thing about this team is that it can hurt you in a lot of ways, which makes us difficult to defend. We have so much motion and so many formations that defenses have trouble preparing for us. They never know what we're going to throw at them. For me, it's like being a kid with a bunch of new toys. You don't know which one to play with next."

Gibbs was very aware of what Theismann meant to the Redskin offense. He realized he had the extra burden of performing with a lot of new players and with formations which were made even more difficult in a strike-shortened season.

"Except for a game or two, Joe has been as consistent as you can want from a quarterback," Gibbs said. "As he goes, we go. It's as simple as that. We've surrounded him with lots of different people, but now he knows who is going to play and when."

Like Theismann, Moseley was also a model of consistency, an attribute the Redskins relied on because they needed his field goal kicking. He was directly responsible for five of Washington's eight victories. He finally earned some national attention after he established a new record for field goal accuracy, breaking Garo Yepremian's record of 20 and, before his string was snapped, adding two more field goals.

"That record means more to me than any other I can think of," Moseley said. "I want to be known for my consistency. It's hard to be more consistent than hitting 21 in a row. I've never felt better at this stage of the season. My leg is strong, and I haven't had any pull problems. There's no reason why I can't kick for a long time to come."

Gibbs wouldn't mind that at all. "He's made of steel," Gibbs said. "I don't know where we'd be without him."

Safety Mark Murphy agreed. "I've seen Mark kick field goals this year in mud, on ice, in the middle of a horrible rainstorm and in snow," Murphy said. "You have the feeling he won't miss. But he's always been that way. There is no one else we'd want to be kicking in pressure situations."

And then there's Riggins. Since Gibbs relied more on the run than the pass this season with a one-back offense for the most part, he designed its effectiveness around Riggins. The emphasis was on ball control; Riggins presented a big, durable back who very rarely fumbled. Now that Riggins was happy, following his year of retirement in 1980, he enjoyed the action. In fact, he told Gibbs early in the week that he wanted the ball more against Detroit.

"I've never felt younger," Riggins said, and he isn't one to talk much. "I've stopped drinking barrels of beer."

Just as long as he doesn't stop running. Despite missing the final regular season game, Riggins carried the ball more than any other back in the NFL during the 1982 campaign. The only fumble he committed came after he carried the ball 318 consecutive times without losing it. The Redskins like to use Riggins a lot during the fourth quarter.

"When we get into the fourth period and we have to have a good drive to win, we have confidence John is going to do the job," said tackle Mark May, one of the Hogs that Riggins runs behind. "It makes our job easier. We just hope his body can take it."

It was unexpected that the Redskins as a team would come this far. After all, they were only an 8-8 team the year before, and none of the experts felt they would do much better with a new coach and new personnel. But Gibbs had more faith in his one-back system which he installed the sixth week of the 1981 season, resulting in the Redskins winning eight of their last eleven games.

"We found if we could control the ball, not make more than two turnovers a game, run consistently and play aggressive defense, we could win," Gibbs reasoned. "We still took our passing shots, but we weren't going to succeed throwing 40 times every game.

"The players learned sometime early in this season that if they kept plugging away, good things would happen. Nothing has come easy. They have had to scratch and scramble every week, but they play very hard. I've never seen a

Although stopped on this play, Riggins finished the game with 119 yards.

Safeties Tony Peters, left, and Mark Murphy, right, make sure Detroit running back Horace King doesn't get up after a spill.

team play near its potential every week as well as this one does. Now they believe in themselves, that they can win. They have confidence, they aren't running scared."

Yet, the normally enthusiastic Theismann appeared quite subdued most of the week. Part of the reason was that he hadn't been getting a normal night's sleep, having been wakened several times by his eleven-year-old son Joey who, like his father, was bothered by a cold. Then, too, Theismann was busier than usual making sure everything was prepared just right for the Lions.

"I've always thought it would be very exciting to be in the NFL playoffs, but it isn't quite the way I imagined," Theismann said. "I've been so busy preparing for Detroit that I haven't thought about this as a playoff game. It's been a busier week than usual because we have one less day to get ready. It seems like any other game, except we know that if we lose, we won't play next week."

That thought didn't escape Gibbs. He wasn't taking the Lions lightly despite their negative record. He left nothing unturned in his final preparations, working with the intensity that he had all season long.

"All I know about Detroit is that they came in here last year, gained a ton of yards, lost by two points and had the ball on the two-yard line when time expired," Gibbs pointed out. "If this game comes down to a field goal, it should be some finish. If it wasn't for the year Mark Moseley has been having, everyone would be talking about their kicker Ed Murray. He missed only one field goal all year."

Actually the last time the Lions beat the Redskins on the road was in Boston in 1935. Before they moved to Washington, they were the Boston Redskins. Since then, the Redskins have played Detroit nine times on the road, and the Lions have been on the losing side every time. This was a very good indication of why the home-field advantage in the playoffs was important.

Although the Lions' quarterback situation was unsettled, they, nevertheless, had stability at running back in Billy Sims. The versatile Sims was the second leading rusher in the NFC, capable of producing the big play either on a run or on the receiving end of a pass. Washington's defensive coordinator, Richie Petitbon, didn't lose sight of that.

"The Lions are very talented, have a great running back in Billy Sims, and their outside receivers can catch the ball," Petitbon said. "They are inconsistent at times, and that's what scares me. You never know if this is the week they will come to play."

The Lions sounded as if they would. Despite a year of inconsistency, in which they had been looked upon as potential Central Division cham-

The veteran Tony Peters calms down rookie Vernon Dean.

pions before the season began, the Lions sounded frisky and seemed eager to challenge the Redskins.

"They show a lot of different blitzes," Hipple noted. "They bring the free safety a lot."

Clark was a little more explicit. "They are very physical," he added. "That Dave Butz is a real load. But I'd say their best pass rusher is Dexter Manley. I hope they blitz a lot. I think we're ready for it."

The Redskins were hoping that Riggins was ready. He figured prominently in their game plan. Since he wanted the ball more often, Gibbs was prepared to give it to him. He looked upon Riggins' request as an indication that the big fullback had recovered completely from the leg injury that caused him to miss the St. Louis game and saw him carry the ball only nine times the week before against New Orleans. Riggins ran gingerly toward the end of the week and didn't appear troubled by his bruised thigh.

Gibbs wasn't counting much on Joe Washington who didn't practice all week because of a painfully swollen knee. The bigger concern was replacing Monk. Gibbs named little Alvin Garrett, who had caught only one pass all season, to replace the star wide receiver.

Theismann wasn't worried. "I don't think this team is the type of team to let injuries affect them," he said.

Manley was much more outspoken. "I think we're going to show the world what the Washington Redskins are all about," exclaimed Manley, who had been overly demonstrative against the Cardinals the previous week and was ejected from the game for fighting. "We haven't gotten any respect. Maybe it's because we've got a lot of young ball players."

Rodney Dangerfield, the comedian whose routine is centered around the line, "I get no respect," must have learned of Manley's lament. He sent a telegram to Theismann which the quarterback shared with his teammates. It read:

I KNOW WHAT IT'S LIKE NOT GETTING ANY RESPECT. GOOD LUCK.

RODNEY DANGERFIELD

The excitement of Washington's first playoff in six years was evident in the attendance. Not a single no-show was recorded, meaning that 55,045 tickets were sold and every one accounted for. The Redskin crowd hardly had a chance to settle down before Detroit took the kickoff to start the game. The Lions started to roar early. Hipple opened the game with a pass to wide receiver Leonard Thompson that gained 12 yards on the Detroit 48. After Sims gained three yards, Dexter Bussey got the Lions a first down with a nine-yard burst to the Washington 40. Hipple then went back to Thompson and connected on a 19-yard pass and another first down on the 21. Detroit was indeed threatening. Just when it appeared that Hipple had solved the Washington defense, linebackers Neal Olkewicz and Rich Milot caused the Lions frustration. Olkewicz jarred the ball loose from Sims and Milot recovered the fumble to give Washington the ball on the 29. Considering the way the Lions were moving, it was a big turnover.

Theismann came out throwing and hit Brown with a 17-yard completion on the 36. After Riggins lost a yard, Theismann tried his passing game again. His first pass to Rick Walker only gained two yards. When he missed the next one to Brown, Jeff Hayes had to punt. The kick only carried 32 yards, and Detroit had good field position at its 36-yard line.

Hipple tried the bomb on first down but underthrew wide receiver Tracy Porter. After Horace King ran for nine yards, Hipple picked up the first down by running for two yards. On the next play, Hipple had the Lions threatening once again. For the third time he connected on a pass with Thompson. This one covered 34 yards and gave Detroit the ball on the Redskin 29. Washington's defense was being tried for the second time.

On first, Dexter Manley held Sims to no gain. Hipple on a keeper picked up six yards to the 23. On third down, Hipple was thinking pass. So was Washington cornerback Jeris White. He had a gut feeling that Hipple would try a quick pass to Sims coming out of the backfield. He was right. White cut in front of Sims and ran 77 yards down the sidelines for a touchdown. That one play seemed to change the tempo of the game after Moseley's kick gave the Redskins a 7-0 lead.

Detroit couldn't do anything following the kickoff. In fact, the tenacious Washington defense came through with another turnover. After Hipple missed on a pass, King picked up four yards. But on third down, cornerback Vernon Dean came on a blitz andf dropped Hipple for a six-yard loss. Hipple lost the ball and tackle Darryl Grant recovered it on the Detroit 19-yard line. The Redskins had an excellent opportunity to score more points.

Theismann put the Lions further in trouble when he fired a seven-yard pass to Walker on the

Wide receiver Alvin Garrett beats Detroit defensive back Bruce McNorton for a touchdown.

12-yard line. After Riggins was stopped short of a first down with only a two-yard gain, the determined fullback broke through for a six-yard advance to the four-yard line. Redskin fans were cheering in anticipation of another touchdown. Suddenly, the Washington attack stalled. Riggins carried twice and couldn't gain a single yard. On third down, Theismann tried a pass to Brown that failed. The Redskins turned to Moseley for a field goal, and he delivered a 26-yard kick that opened Washington's margin to 10-0.

After stopping Detroit on three downs, the Redskins got the ball back for one play before the first period ended. A short punt gave them prime field position on the Detroit 45. Theismann advanced his team further into Detroit territory with a nine-yard pass to diminutive Alvin Garrett who was starting his first game as a Redskin. On the opening play of the second quarter, Riggins broke loose for 11 yards to the 25. After he made four more on the next play, Joe Washington danced for nine yards and another Redskin first down on the 12. The Redskins appeared ready to score again. Riggins got down to the 10. On the next play, Redskin fans moaned when Theismann was sacked for an 11-yard loss back on the 21. Unfazed, Theismann brushed off his pants and called Garrett's number in the huddle. The speedy Garrett got by cornerback Bruce McNorton, and Theismann threw a perfect pass in

The Hogs, led by Jeff Bostic (53) and Russ Grimm (68) hold off the Lions.

Cornerback Jeris White is about to intercept a pass intended for Billy Sims in the first period. White ran it back 77 yards for Washington's first touchdown.

the end zone for a touchdown. Moseley's conversion gave Washington a 17-0 advantage.

Despite being down, Detroit didn't give up. In fact, following the kickoff, they threatened for the third time in the game. The Hipple-Thompson combination puzzled the Washington secondary. First, Hipple found him for a 12-yard gain. Then he timed him perfectly with a 48-yard completion on the Washington 14-yard line. The Redskin defense faced still another challenge. Bussey got down to the ten-yard line. Hipple's quick pass to King reached the five. On third down, Hipple turned to Sims for the touchdown that would get the Lions back into the game. Butz was ready. He hit Sims hard, causing him to fumble for the second time. The ball rolled towards Manley who recovered it on the four. It was another big turnover.

Riggins then got the Redskins out of danger. He carried three consecutive times for seven, 12, and four yards in moving the ball to the 27. After Walker ran for five yards on an end around, Riggins was stopped on third down. Still, it gave Hayes room to punt. Washington got the ball back two minutes later when Detroit couldn't do anything. Kick return ace Mike Nelms gave the

Redskins fine field position when he returned Tom Skladany's punt 39 yards to the Detroit 48.

Walker caught Theismann's pass for a nine-yard gain to the 39. Riggins then got the first down on the 37. Theismann and Garrett hooked up for 12 yards and another first down on the 25. Washington was now in Moseley's range as the first half was nearing its completion. Riggins ran for four yards. After the two-minute warning, Theismann missed on a pass to Garrett. On third down, Theismann came back to Garrett. Again Garrett got open and Theismann found him for his second touchdown pass of the game. Moseley's extra point gave Washington a 24-0 bulge at halftime.

Washington continued its relentless attack after getting the second-half kickoff. It didn't take Theismann long to get the Redskins still another touchdown. He went to work from the 26-yard line and opened with a 20-yard pass to Garrett. Then Riggins rumbled loose. He ran for 25 yards before he was brought down on the Detroit 29. After just two plays, the Redskins were threatening. The next two times, Theismann gave the ball to Riggins. However, after gaining five yards on the first carry, Riggins was dropped for a three-

yard loss back on the 27. Theismann felt it was time to go to Garrett again. Once more Garrett turned on his speed and beat his defender. Theismann hit him on the run with a 27-yard touchdown pass, the third one of the game. Nobody ever imagined that Garrett would replace Monk with such a debut. Moseley converted and Washington was now producing a rout, 31-0.

While Garrett was being congratulated by his teammates on the sidelines, Hipple was trying desperately to rally the Lions. Nothing is more embarrassing to a team than getting routed in a playoff game shown on national television. Relying on his passing for the most part, Hipple led the Lions to their first touchdown on a long 83-yard drive that took 11 plays. Seven of the plays were passes. Hipple completed six of them, the final one a 15-yard touchdown pass to tight end David Hill. Murray kicked the extra point which still left the Lions far behind, 31-7.

Early in the final period the Lions were stirring around at the Washington end of the field. They were hoping to score again and make the point differential a bit more respectable. But White wouldn't have it. He intercepted Hipple's pass on the 20-yard line to send the Lions off the field in disgust.

With some 13 minutes left, it was up to Theismann to use up as much of the clock as possible since the Redskins were safely ahead. He started by handing the ball to Riggins who got five and then four yards. On third down he nodded to Riggins again. Riggins wanted the ball more, and he was getting it. Riggins wore down the Detroit defense by taking off on a 25-yard run to the Lion 46-yard line. When he carried for the fourth straight time, he could only get a yard. Theismann then missed on a pass but kept the drive going by completing a 15-yard toss to Washington on the 30. Riggins got three, but a motion penalty set back the Redskins to the 32. Theismann used his running ability to gain nine yards before stepping out of bounds on the 23. However, on third down, a pass to Walker lost two yards. The Redskins were looking for three more points from Moseley who lined up a 42-yard field goal. His kick had the distance, but not the accuracy as it went off to the right of the goal posts.

It really didn't matter though, except that perhaps Moseley's pride might have been hurt. After the Lions produced a couple of first downs, they were stopped, and Washington got the ball back with 6:23 remaining in the game. Turning to Wilbur Jackson who had replaced Riggins, Theismann ran out the clock. Jackson carried on eight of the ten plays Theismann used in reaching the 14-yard line when time expired. Washington made it look easy, 31-7.

It shouldn't really be a surprise that the Lions only scored once. Washington had allowed a league-low 128 points during the nine-game season, despite the fact that they yielded 34 alone against Philadelphia in the opening game of the campaign. They shut down Sims with only 19 yards in six carries, limiting the entire Detroit ground offensive to just 95 yards. They came up with the big plays on defense and found a new hero in Garrett. Gibbs couldn't have been happier.

"It was a big day for us," Gibbs said. "The playoffs are new for us. Early in the game, with them going up and down the field, I really thought it was going to be blood and guts out there all the way down to the wire. But we got some turnovers to stop them. And once we hit some big plays, it got out of hand. The interception by Jeris got us started. Our defense came on just at the right time, and now we've come to count on them. And we're fortunate to have guys like Alvin stepping in there to make big plays.

"I figured everyone would ask me why we haven't been playing Alvin more. Everyone is just picking each other up. When Art gets hurt, Alvin steps in. When John was hurt for a couple of weeks, Joe Washington and Clarence Harmon picked up the load. Now John comes back and we can rest the others. It's been that kind of a year. I just hope we can make it last a few more weeks."

Among the other heroes of the game, Theismann, Riggins and White, Garrett was the most unlikely. Since he signed as a free agent with the Redskins in November of 1981, he had caught only one pass. Against Detroit, he caught six passes for 110 yards and three touchdowns! Before this day he was used primarily on special teams. This day he was special. The hero treatment was new to him.

"I was just lucky," Garrett smiled. "I wouldn't have gotten to play if Art hadn't been injured. No, I never thought about catching three touchdown passes. You dream about it, but this time it came true. I'm going to get talked about at practice on Monday because I didn't block today. They're going to say I'm getting soft because I'm a wide receiver. This is my best day in professional football, but I still prefer the special teams. I have to say that, if I want my special team coach Wayne Sevier to still talk to me. He's the only rea-

Alvin Garrett, one of the game's heroes, scores his third touchdown of the game in the third quarter on a 27-yard pass from Joe Theismann.

son I'm with the Redskins."

Theismann doesn't believe that at all. He had a good day passing, 14 of 19 for 210 yards and three touchdowns and wasn't surprised by Garrett's performance.

"Garrett wouldn't be in this league unless he could perform," Theismann said. "Alvin finally got his chance to play. The little guy filled in and did a great job. He hasn't been there as wide receiver all season. He was thrown into a difficult situation and looked as though he didn't miss a beat. Alvin is a great athlete with great moves. With our style of offense, we don't have just 11 offensive players. We have 15 or 18 guys who can do the job, and he made the most of his opportunity. They all get time during practice during the week.

"Today I wasn't looking for Alvin. We take what the defense dictates. He made some great catches, and he made some great moves to get open. Any word short of 'great' wouldn't do Alvin justice. It was not an easy game. They came at us at the beginning, and we hung in there. They started to blitz and pressure our outside receivers, and it's up to us to beat that. It's the best team effort we've had in three or four weeks.

"But overall, it was the offensive line that dictated the ebb and flow of the game. We didn't design our offense toward any individual. You take what the defense gives us. They gave Alvin that bump and run, and he beat his guy at it."

The same way White beat Hipple. His first-period interception was a big one. Detroit was moving, and it appeared as if the Lions were heading for a touchdown. Instead, he turned the interception into a Washington touchdown.

"I'm supposed to make it look like I'm going with the wide receiver," White explained about stepping in front of Sims coming out of the backfield. "Then I fall off. I don't think Hipple saw me. He threw it just as I made my move. I didn't think I was going to get it. I thought I would just knock it down. But I tipped it in the air and was able to get it.

"Wow, 77 yards. Was it that long? I thought I was out of shape because I had to sit out the next play to catch my breath. All the way downfield, I kept thinking there's got to be a flag. When I got into the end zone, I sort of looked around to see if everything was okay. 'Hey,' I said to myself, 'it's a touchdown.'"

Although Riggins didn't score a touchdown, he, too, had a big day. Coming off an injury, he carried the ball 25 times and gained 119 yards, which is an average of 4.8 yards a run. As usual, Riggins didn't talk to the writers about his play, which came against the best rushing defense in the league.

"John doesn't have to talk to me, either," Gibbs said. "But on Thursday he came up and said, 'I want the ball on Saturday.' So we gave it to him."

Clark, who had said earlier in the week that "the Redskins are not a great team," refused to alter his opinion. "I still feel the same way," he said. "They are a good, solid club and are well-coached. I'm not taking anything away from them. They could win it all."

Even All-Pro defensive tackle Doug English remained unconvinced about the Redskins' performance. "You know the expression," English said, "we didn't get beat, we just ran out of time'? Well, I'd like to line up and play them again right now. They're not a 31-7 better team than we are."

The respect for the Redskins still wasn't there. Redskin fans couldn't have cared less that evening. Instead, some were more concerned about ordering a Number Seven sandwich in Theismann's Falls Church, Virginia, restaurant. They were waiting in line to eat the tasty roast beef sandwich with Swiss cheese, cole slaw and Russian dressing. The price was right, too, $3.75. Inside, Theismann was celebrating at a back table with some of his family and friends.

"Here's to our continued success," Theismann toasted. "To money in our pockets. And to rings on our fingers."

"And bells on our toes," Moseley added.

"And to straightening out our field goal kicker," Theismann laughed.

The night was theirs to enjoy.... ●

JANUARY 8, 1983
AT RFK STADIUM, WASHINGTON, D.C.
NFC FIRST-ROUND PLAYOFF GAME

Detroit	0	0	7	0	— 7
Washington	10	14	7	0	— 31

W—White, 77 interception return (Moseley kick)

W—FG, Moseley, 26

W—Garrett, 21 pass from Theismann (Moseley kick)

W—Garrett, 21 pass from Theismann (Moseley kick)

W—Garrett, 27 pass from Theismann (Moseley kick)

D—Hill, 15 pass from Hipple (Murray kick)

A couple of Joes got the Redskins on their way.

MINNESOTA PLAYOFF

"We're Just Now Learning How To Win"

Minnesota's stoic coach, Bud Grant, made Redskin hearts happy. One thing Grant has in common with the Redskins and their fans is his hatred of the Dallas Cowboys. In fact, Grant was quite vocal about it the day after the Vikings defeated the Atlanta Falcons to advance to round two of the NFC playoffs against the Redskins in Washington. Even before anything was said or written about the game itself, Grant began his harangue of the Cowboys in far off Eden Prairie, Minnesota, where the Vikings had enjoyed the luxury of a domed stadium for the first season in their history. It only emphasized that Grant's bitterness was not the result of the cold Minnesota winters but of a genuine dislike for the Cowboys. His contempt was heard not only around Washington, but more than likely as far away as Dallas. He also had a little anger left to make his feelings known about Miami's Don Shula and the television industry.

One would think that Grant would have been happy at this point of the season. After all, the Vikings burned the Cowboys, 31-27 in the final Monday Night Game of the year, finishing with a 5-4 record and a spot in the playoffs. The 30-24 victory over the Falcons in the first round of the playoffs was Minnesota's fourth win in their last five games. Such a roll should make any coach happy. Grant apparently wanted to get a few things off his chest regarding the Cowboys and the NFL itself. When Grant has strong feelings about something, he wasn't afraid to make them known. In Super Bowl VIII he complained to league officials that the training facilities they reserved for Minnesota in Houston were old and inadequate; he even showed reporters a nest of pigeons who had made their home in the dressing room.

Grant was heard even before the 1982 season began. The Vikings were scheduled to play the Baltimore Colts in the annual Hall of Fame game in Canton, Ohio. One day Grant will gain entrance into the Hall as one of pro football's winningest coaches. But, he used that particular game to make another point, one that may have far-reaching effects in the future. Grant felt that the coaches of both teams should be paid along with the players. To make the point more dramatic, he threatened to boycott the game with his staff. After he got his point across,* he relented and the game went on as scheduled.

Before he started to prepare the Vikings for the Saturday game against the Redskins, Grant had a few more complaints.

"Since Dallas is the league's team, it will play on Sunday this week," Grant began. "Everybody feels he wants to see the league's team. Of course, that

Quarterback Joe Theismann has a lot of protection as he prepares to pass against Minnesota.

also means the league's team will have an extra day to heal injuries. They seem to get a lot of things their way.''

He didn't have to be reminded that Tex Schramm, the president of the Cowboys, is on the NFL Competition Committee. He went even further, disclosing that he had given considerable thought to the matter.

"Tex Schramm is a good buddy of Pete Rozelle," Grant continued. "There's nothing the matter with that. Pete has to have some sounding boards. But we stated early in the year that the Competition Committee is a very strong committee. Don Shula is on the Competition Committee, and two days after New England uses a tractor to clear the snow against Miami, we get a four-page directive on what to do about snow. We've been dealing with snow and ice since 1961, and with all the problems other teams had with the weather, too. Something happened to Don Shula before all those directives and specifications were issued. When you're on the Competition Committee, you get a lot of action.

"Tex Schramm has been trying to move playoff games from cold-weather sites to warm-weather sites. I hope his influence doesn't get that one through. I didn't make this observation, but someone else did regarding the extra games played on January 2 and 3. Of the four teams with representatives on the Competition Committee, Miami played winless Baltimore; Cincinnati played lowly Houston; Atlanta faced New Orleans and Dallas played us. Dallas had another patsy, at least it thought so. The result kind of fooled them. But they had a lot more success when it came to the television schedule the first week of the playoffs. Our game was shown in Atlanta, Minnesota, Northern Alabama and Puerto Rico. Dallas went everywhere else. Obviously the TV people prefer Dallas. But TV determines most of that. They pay the bucks and they call the shots. Maybe Dallas works hard at creating that image and getting exposure."

At first it seemed that Grant was using psychology in getting the Redskins themselves to think about Dallas and look past the Vikings. Coaches have used such tactics in the past, and Grant was reminded about it.

"Ah, I'm just sick and tired of talking about who's hurt and who's not hurt," Grant said. "It's part of my job to sell the product, and you guys need something to write. I'll talk about the Redskins tomorrow after I have seen films of their recent games. I've only seen one reel of their film, and I didn't see them against Detroit on Satur-

John Riggins runs past Vikings' John Swain
116 *on the way to another 100-yard game.*

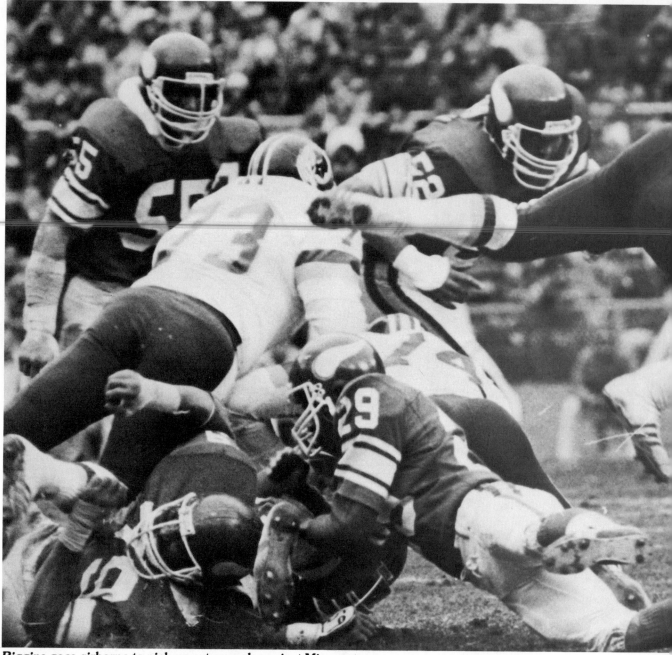

Riggins goes airborne to pick up extra yards against Minnesota.

day. I'm not familiar with them at all. There are a lot of names I have to get straight. We were supposed to play Washington on November 14 but we didn't do any preparing for them because of the strike.

"Washington, though, is a lot like us. They use two tight ends a lot, and use a lot of motion. But they probably go deep a lot more than some teams. They have some wide receivers who can really run. There's not a great deal of difference in our team since we last played the Redskins two

years ago. Our defense has a little more maturity. We have a little more speed in the secondary, and Charlie Johnson, whom we got from the Eagles, is a good addition at nose tackle. Offensively, we're very similar, but maybe we're having a little more success because we got involved in the wide-open offense before everyone else. It's just that we're not a dominant team anymore. It used to be we could count on just beating other teams. Not now."

For someone who has been called "The Ice-

man of Minnesota," Grant had a great deal to say. Like Gibbs, Grant is also innovative and has been one of the more successful coaches in the NFL. In his 16 years at Minnesota, his teams have won 152 games and appeared in four Super Bowls. If he is unfulfilled as a coach, it is because he has never won a Super Bowl. Nevertheless, Gibbs admires Grant.

"The man has been a winner his entire career," Gibbs said. "A lot of people shoot up or shoot down. But the way you really judge a coach in this league is when after ten years you sustain a winning program."

Certainly Gibbs has done just that this season and part of last. The past year and a half, the Redskins have been the hottest team in the NFL. During that time, they won 12 of 13 games. Since the Vikings won four of their last five, their meeting on Saturday was to be between two hot teams seeking to advance to the championship game the following week. The winner would face the survivor of the Green Bay-Dallas contest

Tight end Don Warren scores Redskins' first touchdown on a three-yard pass from Joe Theismann.

which was scheduled in Dallas on Sunday.

"We're just now learning how to win," Moseley said. "We're putting everything together—players, coaches, philosophies."

That's the way it looked, too. Offensively and defensively, Washington was indeed coming together. The Redskins ranked fourth in total offense in the NFC and second in defense. In their last five games, the Redskin defense allowed only 38 points. No one did better than that. Much of the preparation for the Vikings was planned after the coaches spent hours reviewing Minnesota game films. Assistant coach Dan Henning studied the defensive tendencies while defensive coordinator Richie Petitbon concerned himself with the offensive trends.

"What we don't like is change," Henning said. "What we like, we keep in. But everything is tested thoroughly before it is used in a game. For example, we may want to run a certain play against two different defenses. Before the week is out, we'll make sure we try it that way in practice. If we've prepared adequately during the week, there is no need to vary from the plan. It comes

down to this. We try to predict, when things are on the line, what the other team will do. The closer we are to being right those times, the more successful we'll be."

Theismann reported to practice an hour early each day. He studied the game plan hard, reviewing it at least three times a day. He wanted to eliminate any doubts on his part as he was the one who had to execute the attack against the Vikings. Washington was only two games away from Pasadena and Super Bowl XVII. He wanted to be there.

"A lot of information is familiar, but Joe Gibbs must be the father of invention," Theismann said. "He uses the game plan every week to challenge us with something new. It keeps things exciting."

It is much the same way on defense. The Redskins play it excitingly.

"We always put in more alignments than we think we will need," Petitbon said, "because you never are sure what you are going to need. You think you've anticipated but sometimes the game unfolds differently and you wind up relying more on one defense than you thought. We've got one

Free safety Mark Murphy puts a halt on Viking wide receiver Sam McCullum.

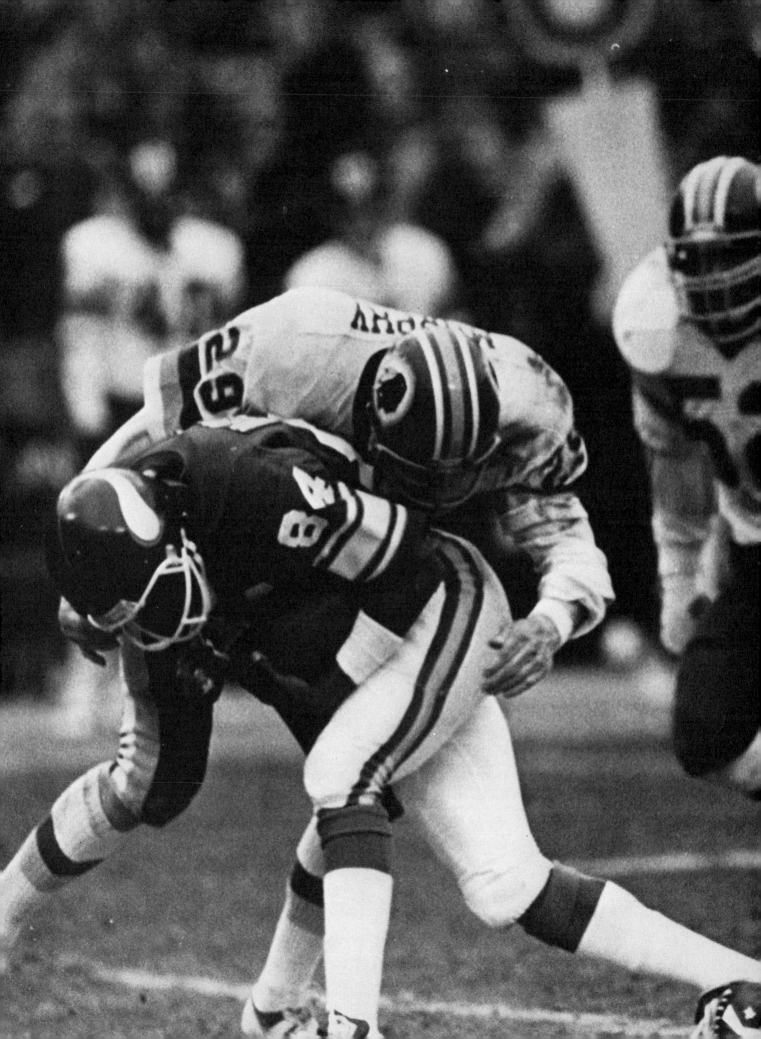

blitz that we've practiced for 12 weeks now and haven't used yet."

Like Theismann on offense, safety Mark Murphy is responsible for carrying out the defensive game plan. He calls the signals in the defensive huddle.

"If we aren't comfortable with something, we'll say so," Murphy revealed. "The coaches are very good at listening to us and making adjustments. They realize we are the ones who have to execute it. I don't know if we'll have the best record in the NFC every year, but I think we're going to continue to make the playoffs. We've laid a foundation for the future."

However, the immediate concern was the Vikings. The Redskins would like to forget the last time they faced Minnesota in Washington. It was in 1980 and the Vikings trampled the Redskins 39-14. Minnesota had also won the teams' only playoff encounters, 27-20 in 1973 and 35-20 in 1976. Both these games were played in Minnesota's Metropolitan Stadium before the Vikings moved into their new domed stadium this year. Obviously, the Vikings are a much stronger team when playing at home. They emerged victorious only once in their last nine road games.

"I don't know why we play better at home," said Viking quarterback Tommy Kramer. "I guess you perform better in more comfortable surroundings. But, regardless, I don't think that that should have much effect in the playoffs. Everybody knows it's the last shot. The effort will be there.

"What we have to do is to control the ball and keep their offense from getting it. We can't give up points like we have on interceptions. Our defense has to shut down their passing game and put pressure on Theismann."

Kramer's attempt at ball control was made more difficult because of the loss of his star wide receiver Ahmad Rashad. Until he injured his back the last Sunday in December, Rashad had been one of the Vikings' leading receivers. The injury sidelined him for the rest of the season. Still, Kramer was relieved that the club's top pass catcher, Sammy White, would be back in the line-up after missing the Atlanta game. His only other concern was running back Ted Brown, who was troubled by a shoulder injury. Kramer's other main receiver, tight end Joe Senser, was healthy after a nagging injury and showed his readiness with six receptions against the Falcons. Kramer was as important to Minnesota's attack as Theismann was to Washington's. Both excelled at executing the short passing game, and each had a

Ted Brown (23) finds there is nowhere to go against the Redskin defense.   123

strong enough arm to go deep. Kramer made use of seven different receivers to cach 122 or more passes in spreading the offense around.

"I would say Theismann is more versatile than a guy like Danny White because he can run and scramble, and they protect him a lot," said Viking linebacker Matt Blair, the team's defensive captain. "He's a very good quarterback and makes their offense go."

It had been evident against Detroit the previous game. Riggins returned to action for the first time in almost two weeks and ran for 119 yards on 26 carries, giving no indication that his injured thigh was bothering him. Even more remarkable was the way Theismann synchronized with wide receiver Alvin Garrett, who was sent into the Redskin offense as a replacement for the injured Art Monk, the team's leading receiver. Theismann completed six passes to Garrett for 116 yards and three touchdowns. His first two touchdown passes of 21 yards looked like an instant replay. They were executed with such timing that nobody would have believed that Garrett was starting his first game of the year.

"The little guy filled in and did a great job," Theismann said. "He hasn't been there at wide receiver all season. He was thrown into a difficult situation and looked as though he didn't miss a beat."

Offensive tackle George Starke took it all in stride. He didn't seem excited like some of his teammates, probably because as a veteran, he was there in 1972 at Super Bowl VII when Washington lost to Miami 14-7. He was treating the playoffs as if they were regular season games.

"It's just one football game, the same as any other one," Starke said. "We have to prepare for it the way we'd prepare for any other game and

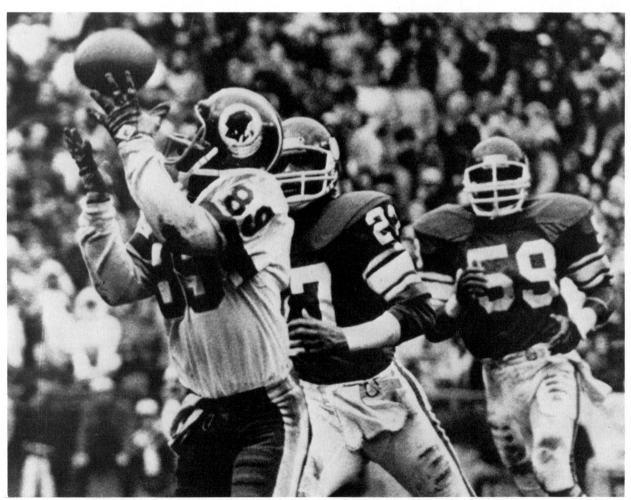

Wide receiver Alvin Garrett grabs Joe Theismann's 18-yard touchdown pass to score Washington's third touchdown of the game.

Riggins finds some daylight in middle of Minnesota line.

play it like it was a game against them six weeks ago. You can't go crazy because it's a playoff game. You have to keep doing what you're good at and not think about the fact that there's a chance it'll be the last game of the season.

"This team isn't much different than the one in 1972, except it is much younger. Those guys were tough, a wonderful blend of misfits and malcontents, guys like Pat Fischer, Ron McDole and Diron Talbert. It was like *True Grit*. These guys are tough, too, but young tough, full of energy and enthusiasm. This team has just as much character as that one."

Yet, they weren't anything like the Hogs. They were dearly loved by Redskin fans in the same way as "The Over The Hill Gang." But the Hogs were something else, and they were embraced by Redskin fans after seeing what the offensive line did for Riggins. On game day, they let a national television audience know how much they loved their Hogs. There were signs all over RFK Stadium that read: "We're Hog Wild Over the Redskins"; "We're in Hog Heaven"; "The Hogs That Ate Minnesota"; and "Hogtie The Vikings". Any hog farmer in America would have loved it.

There was one more banner that perhaps said it all: "We Want the Cowboys."

But first the Redskins had to get past the Vikings. Safety Tony Peters put it on the line when he said, "We're only as good as our last game." It served as a warning.

Surprisingly, all the seats were not filled in RFK Stadium. Although the game was sold out, some 452 ticketholders were missing. However, the 54,593 who showed up that cloudy day weren't too cold because the game-time temperature was

Riggins scores Washington's second touchdown in first period by powering his way from the two-yard line.

44 degrees. The only cause of discomfort was a 19 MPH wind that occasionally whipped through the stadium.

As the game began it appeared to bother Minnesota kicker Rick Danmeir. The Redskins had won the coin flip and elected to receive the opening kickoff. Danmeir's kick didn't go deep. Wilbur Jackson caught it on the 16 and returned it 18 yards to the Washington 34. Theismann had a good vantage point from which to open his attack. He started it with Riggins. First he got two yards and three more to the 39. It still left the Redskins five yards short of a first down. On the obvious passing down, Riggins left the field and

was replaced by Nick Giaquinto who contributed immediately. Theismann threw him a 17-yard pass on the Minnesota 44-yard line.

Riggins returned to the lineup but Theismann decided to pass again. He did so successfully, hitting Brown with a 12-yard aerial on the Viking 32-yard line. The Redskins were moving. Theismann felt it was time to use Riggins again. He did so almost to the point of stubbornness. Riggins carried the ball five straight times. The first time he got loose for 15 yards to the 17. Then he bulled his way for nine more to the eight. At worse, the Redskins had a field goal ahead of them. Riggins kept running. He carried three

more times and reached the three-yard line. On third down, Theismann switched. He faked a handoff to Riggins, turned and fired a quick three-yard touchdown pass to tight end Don Warren. Theismann made it look easy. The 66-yard drive that took ten plays consumed almost six minutes of a well-executed ball control drive in which Riggins carried the ball seven times. Moseley accounted for the extra point, and Washington led 7-0.

On Minnesota's first offensive series, it was evident that the game plan was to throw against Washington. Kramer dropped back three times to pass and came up empty. However, Viking punt-er Greg Coleman got off a 61-yard punt that rolled dead on the Washington 22-yard line, bringing a bit of joy to the Viking bench.

Theismann began his second possession the same way he did the first. Twice, instead of passing, Theismann kept the ball himself and scampered for six yards and a first down to the 35. He kept the ball again on the next play but could only get a yard because when he tried to pass he couldn't find a receiver open. He attempted to pass on second down but missed, overthrowing Garrett near the sidelines. Theismann had to pass once more. He looked for Warren but threw a little high. The ball went off Warren's stretching fingertips and landed in the arms of Minnesota cornerback John Swain. The Vikings had the ball back on their own 44-yard line.

Minnesota's first running play didn't get much yardage. Middle linebacker Neal Olkewicz stopped Ted Brown as soon as he reached the 45. Kramer went back to his passing game. It still wasn't effective. He missed on two more attempts, running his streak to five straight without a completion. Again Minnesota had to punt.

When Theismann came back on the field, the ball was on the 29-yard line. He switched from the run on the first down and completed a six-yard pass to tight end Rick Walker on the 35. When Riggins gained eight yards, the Redskins had a first down on the 43. Then, Theismann caught the Viking defense by surprise. In what appeared to be a routine running play, he handed the ball to Riggins. Moving straight ahead, Riggins stopped just before he reached the line of scrimmage, turned completely around and lateraled the ball back to Theismann. With no defensive linemen near him, since they were committed to stopping Riggins, Theismann was all alone waiting for Garrett to get open. He did and Theismann lofted a 46-yard pass that the little receiver caught on the Viking 11-yard line. The crowd loved the trickery that fooled the Vikings.

It was time to put Riggins to work again. On his first carry he got five yards, then three. However, on third and two, he carried for a third straight time and only got a yard. It was decision time. On fourth down, they needed a yard for a first down. Gibbs had the choice of going for it or sending in Moseley for an easy field goal that would give the Redskins a 10-0 lead.

He didn't hesitate in his decision. He kept Moseley on the sidelines and signaled Theismann to go for it. The crowd cheered the strategy. They knew it would be Riggins again. Theismann gave him a clean handoff, and Riggins, running hard, broke through the Viking line and got into the end zone. Redskin fans stood cheering as Riggins calmly returned to the bench. Moseley added the conversion and Washington moved into a 14-0 lead with only a minute remaining in the first period. The 71-yard drive took almost four minutes and of the seven plays it required, Riggins carried five times. He was being used extensively and had already run 14 times and produced 59 yards. And, with the Redskins in front, it would appear that Riggins would be asked to carry the ball even more.

Since the Vikings had fallen behind, it was also expected that Kramer would throw more. After

128

The arms of Minnesota's defensive end Mark Mullaney can't stop Riggins.

Brown picked up four yards to the 27, Kramer completed his first pass. On the last play of the first quarter, Kramer completed a ten-yard pass to wide receiver Sam McCullum on the 37. The successful maneuver produced the Vikings' initial first down of the game, an indication of how much Washington dominated the game.

The second period didn't start too encouragingly for Kramer. The first two passes he threw were incomplete. However, he came through with a big third down pass that gave the Vikings a lift. Throwing deep, Kramer connected with wide receiver Terry LeCount on the Washington 21. The play covered 42 yards and gave the Vikings their first scoring opportunity. Kramer continued to throw and hit Brown with a quick three-yard pass. He had the Redskin defense thinking pass and then crossed them up. Brown slipped through the Washington line, broke loose in the secondary and made it safely into the end zone on an 18-yard touchdown run. Danmeir's extra point cut Washington's lead in half, 14-7.

After the kickoff, Theismann didn't waste any time getting a drive started. He opened with an 11-yard pass to Garrett on the 41-yard line. Next it was Riggins. He ran for nine yards and then two more and a first down on the Minnesota 48. Theismann passed to Brown for four yards but a ten-yard penalty on Walker for illegal use of hands set the Redskins back on their 46. Riggins then went out on a pass play but Theismann sent Brown deep and hit him with a 30-yard pass on the Minnesota 24.

The large crowd was anticipating another score. Riggins kept them thinking that way by gaining six yards to the 18-yard line. The Redskins were certainly in Moseley's range now but Theismann was thinking touchdown first. He decided to go to Garrett, his hot receiver. Garrett broke downfield quickly, got a couple of steps on his defender, reached out and caught Theismann's 18-yard pass for a touchdown. Moseley kicked the extra point to restore Washington's 14 point lead, 21-7.

Wide receiver Alvin Garrett scores Washington's third touchdown on an 18-yard pass from Joe Theismann in the second period.

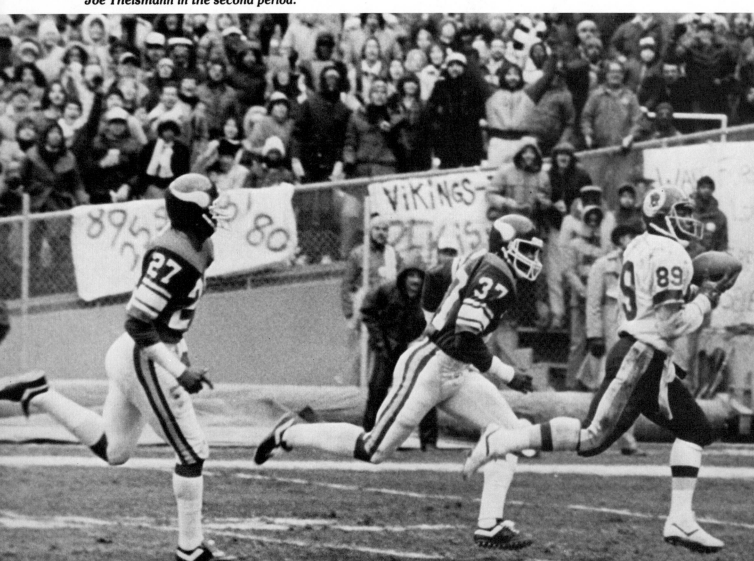

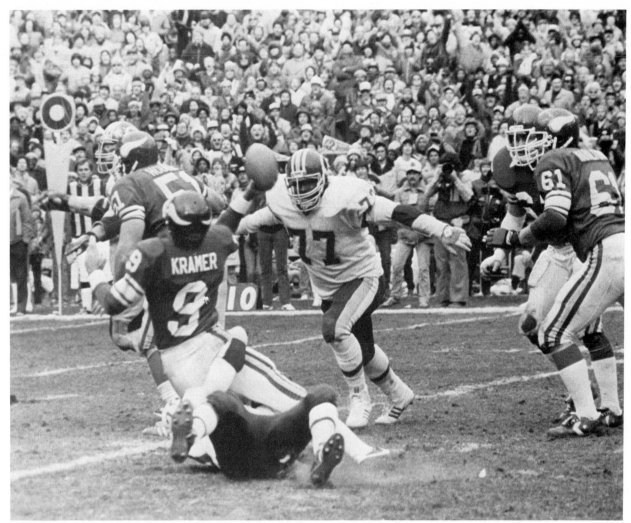

Minnesota quarterback Tommy Kramer desperately tries to pass while caught in the grasp of a Redskin as Darryl Grant moves in to make sure Kramer doesn't get away.

Still, Minnesota didn't appear discouraged. Kramer got the Vikings moving after the kickoff from the 14-yard line. A quick pass to wide receiver Steve Jordan got three yards. A similar one to Brown was stopped for no gain. Sammy White then caught his first pass of the contest, a 13-yard one that gave the Vikings a first down on 30. After Brown failed to gain a yard, Kramer completed a pass to Jordan for eight yards and another one to LeCount for five and a first down on the 43. Kramer wanted to throw again. Tight end Joe Senser ran a crossing pattern deep in the Washington secondary. Kramer threw on the break and Senser caught a 32-yard pass on the Redskin 25.

Kramer hurried the Vikings out of the huddle. He had another pass play called. However, Jeris White made illegal contact with Sammy White and the Redskins were penalized five yards. With

the ball on the 20, Kramer switched to the run. Dave Butz foiled the effort by stopping Brown on the line of scrimmage. Kramer had to pass. Twice he threw to White and both times Dean successfully rejected the play. There was nothing left for the Vikings except a field goal attempt. Danmeir got it off from the 38-yard line. The ball had the distance but hit the left upright and bounced harmlessly to the ground.

There was 3:24 left in the first half when Washington took over. After Riggins was dropped for a yard loss, Joe Washington broke away for 11 yards and a first down on the 30-yard line. Theismann came to the sidelines at the two-minute warning. He conferred with Gibbs. The thinking was that Theismann had enough time to work the ball into field goal range for Moseley rather than just running out the clock. Theismann went to work. His first pass to Walker gained nine yards. When Riggins was turned back in his attempt to get a first down, Theismann went back to the air. He threw six yards to Walker and another first down on the 45.

Theismann called a time out and again he talked with Gibbs. When he returned to the huddle, Giaquinto was there waiting. It was his play. Giaquinto broke out of the backfield and grabbed a 22-yard pass from Theismann on the Minnesota 35. Theismann called time for the third straight time. Only 13 seconds remained, time for one more pass. Theismann couldn't complete it and with the incompletion the clock stopped with eight seconds left. It was Moseley's turn. He lined up a 47-yard field goal. He got the kick off but it went wide to the left. There wouldn't be any more points for the Redskins in the first half. They had to be content with a 21-7 edge.

The Redskins dominated the action during the first half. They had the ball almost 19 minutes during which time they ran off 40 plays to Minnesota's 25; produced a big difference in total yardage, 280 to 147; and had a distinct edge in first downs, 16 to 7. Riggins was involved in just about half the plays, carrying 19 times for 75 yards behind the Hogs.

The Vikings tried to make things happen after receiving the second-half kickoff. They opened with a ground attack. Brown got nine yards and Rickey Young six for a first down on the 35. After Brown was stopped for no gain, Kramer returned to his air attack. He missed on his first pass but then completed one to wide receiver Harold Jackson for 14 yards and a first down on the 49-yard line. Kramer missed again. Rookie Darrin Nelson then ran for four yards. An offside penalty on Dexter Manley gave the Vikings a third and one on the 42. Brown provided the first down when he got to the 41.

Minnesota tried to pull a trick play on the Redskins but the strategy backfired. Kramer lateraled the ball to his tight end Joe Senser, coming around on a reverse. Senser couldn't handle the errant toss. He managed to recover the loose ball on the Viking 41. Brown more than got it back on the next play when he ran for 17 yards to the Redskin 39. Still, Kramer had to pass on third down but couldn't connect with McCullum. Coleman's punt pinned the Redskins on their eight-yard line.

Washington looked to Riggins to run them out of danger. He got four yards and then five, but on a third and one on the 17, he failed to get the first down. Jeff Hayes came in to punt for the first

Viking linebacker Scott Studwell puts an arm lock on Riggins.

time but his kick only went 34 yards to the Viking 49 which gave Minnesota excellent field position. Kramer got them moving right away with a 19-yard pass to McCullum on the Redskin 32. After Tony Galbreath ran for four yards, the Redskin secondary braced for Kramer's passing attack from the 28-yard line. Manley applied pressure, and Kramer's second down pass to Nelson was incomplete. On third down, Kramer passed into the end zone to White, who was open. Washington got a break, however, when the ball went through White's hand. The Vikings decided against a field goal try. Instead, Kramer tried to hit McCullum with a fourth down pass but Joe Lavender, who came in as a fifth defensive back, broke up the play.

Washington took over with almost six minutes left in the third period. They opened with an end around. Theismann handed to Riggins who, in turn, gave the ball to Garrett. The play worked for five yards but a face-mask penalty gave the Redskins a first down on the 37-yard line. Rig-

gins kept the ball the next time and got away for 12 yards before he was brought down on the 49. After Riggins gained two yards and a pass to Warren added two more, Theismann came back to Warren with a nine-yard aerial that gave the Redskins a first down on the Viking 38.

Theismann then gave the ball to Riggins for the twenty-fifth time. Riggins responded for nine yards which gave him 107 for the game. Mixing his plays, Theismann then completed a nine-yard pass to Brown and a first down on the 20. Once again, the Redskins were in Moseley's range. Riggins got it closer with an eight-yard pick up to the 12. Looking to pass, Theismann scrambled out of the pocket and was dropped for no gain. On third down, Theismann tried a pass to Giaquinto but it went incomplete. Moseley entered the game and booted a 29-yard field goal. However, a ten-yard holding penalty on Milot nullified the points. Moseley had to try again from the 39-yard line, and much to the chagrin of the crowd, he missed. After Brown carried for a yard, the third period

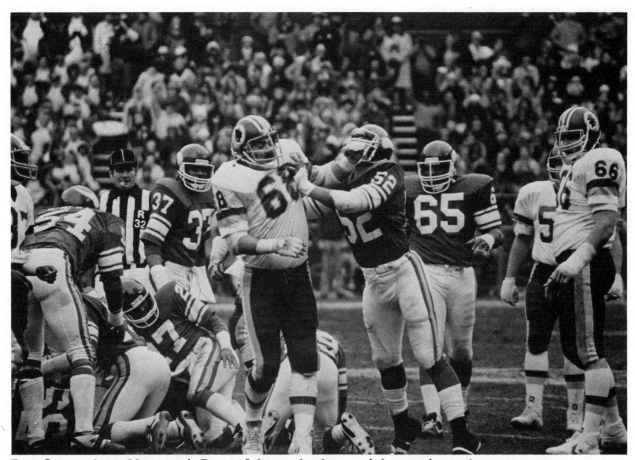

Russ Grimm shows Minnesota's Dennis Johnson that he wasn't happy about what was going on.

Defensive end Tony McGee corrals Minnesota's Tommy Kramer.

action ended. By now the Redskins' fans were chanting, "We Want Dallas!"

When the final quarter opened, Kramer was faced with putting a long drive together to get the Vikings closer. A 13-yard pass to Brown gave the Vikings a first down on the 36. Brown managed two more yards before Kramer went up top. He missed his first pass but on the third down, he connected with LeCount for a first down on the 48. He didn't complete one of his next two passes to LeCount. Then he turned to McCullum and threw a 34-yard aerial that carried the Vikings to

the Redskin 18-yard line. Minnesota was applying pressure now.

Brown got down to the 14, but the Vikings made a mistake. They were caught on a holding penalty which set them back to the 23-yard line. The Redskins were ready for Kramer's passes. A holding penalty on the first one pushed the Vikings back to the 33. A Kramer to Brown pass got only four yards. He came right back to Brown and gained 14 yards to the 15. On fourth down, the Vikings elected to go for it. Tony McGee was ready. He broke through and sacked Kramer for

The Vikings tried everything to stop Riggins, even to the point of Charlie Johnson trying to pull Riggins' shirt off. Riggins finished with an unbelievable 185 yards for the game.

a six-yard loss.

There was 10:15 left when the Redskins got the ball. They specifically wanted to control the ball as much as possible and that meant giving it to Riggins. He carried four straight times and gained a total of 27 yards. When they couldn't get another first down, Hayes punted. By now, there was only 5:39 remaining in the game. Minnesota could only manage one first down before they were forced to punt.

At 4:17, the Redskins got the ball back on their own 28-yard line. The crowd was yelling for Riggins. After the first play, they shouted louder. The seemingly inexhaustible fullback rambled for 29 yards to the Viking 43 before he was dragged down. He kept on running. Two yards, six yards, three yards, a one-yard loss and finally four more yards before he was taken out of the game with 1:05 on the clock. Riggins received a standing ovation, and he responded in a manner never seen before. First, he removed his helmet and bowed to one side of the stadium and then to the other. The fans were still applauding when their hero reached the Redskin bench for more praise from his teammates. With only one play remaining, Theismann dropped to one knee to seal the 21-7 victory. The Redskins were one step closer to Pasadena on the powerful legs of Riggins. The mighty fullback defied all odds. He carried the ball a phenomenal 37 times and ran for an unbelievable 185 yards. Nothing fancy, but a display of power reminiscent of the old days of professional football. His yardage established a new playoff record.

Gibbs couldn't contain his praise. He was almost ecstatic.

"John is stupendous," Gibbs exclaimed. "He is really remarkable. For a 33-year-old, he is amazing. He said two weeks ago that he was excited about the playoffs. He told me then that he felt real good. If he says he's going to do something, he does it. He says he doesn't have many years left, but he's got me convinced otherwise. I thank God for John Riggins, and all the other players we have here.

"We're thrilled to be where we are at this time. We're happy that we can sit back tomorrow and watch the other game on television. We know whoever is coming next week is going to be good. We're certainly glad to be playing here. We played hard and consistent today. It was a total team effort. We had some drives that ate up a lot of time. Keeping the ball and eating up the clock were important for us. I don't know what, time or possession, but it had to be a factor. We sure

didn't feel at all comfortable with a 21-7 lead."

Grant also found time to laud Riggins. He had admired Riggins for a number of years when he played for the New York Jets.

"I wined him and dined him when he was a free agent in 1975, but the Redskins offered him more money," Grant said. "John Riggins has been doing that for a lot of years. He did a good job and got a lot of help from the offensive line. That's the kind of game we didn't want to get into against Washington. When they got 14 points ahead they were content to run the ball. We tried different things to stop Riggins, but he had people who did the blocking. It doesn't matter what you do, people have to block, and Riggins has that strong upfield speed."

It was "The Hogs" who made it happen. Grant knew it. Yet, he didn't realize the Washington offensive line had gone into the game with an added incentive.

"The line wanted to block for John because of some of the things the Minnesota players had said earlier in the week," disclosed guard Russ Grimm. "They said we were big and slow. We took that as a challenge. A handshake from Riggo is like 50,000 people cheering for you. You love to block for him. Last week he sat in the offensive line meeting with us. He's really down to earth. He could be wearing three-piece suits with the money he makes, but he just dresses in camouflage pants."

Another Hog, center Jeff Bostic, made Riggins' performance sound easy. "With us, it's Riggo right, Riggo left and Riggo up the middle," he said. "He's our only running back, and it's nothing very fancy. But he has such great quickness for a guy his size, and he's so very, very strong."

Theismann, who had another good playoff game, 17 of 23 passing for 212 yards and two touchdowns, also appreciated Riggins' efforts. It definitely made Theismann's job easier.

"I certainly have no complaints about that kind of day," Theismann said. "With Riggins running the way he was, there were 37 or 38 guys on the Vikings who never knew what we were going to

do. That made it easy for me. It's really a treat to watch him, and I had the greatest seat in the house. He's a champion. The reason the flea flicker worked so well was because it came off a formation Riggins had been getting a lot of yards on. John nearly kept the ball instead of giving it back to me because he had such a big hole in front of him.

"Our fans want Dallas next week. That was obvious when they started yelling for them in the third quarter. But I don't really care. Somebody is going to have to come to us."

Owner Jack Kent Cooke came by Theismann's locker. The quarterback looked up and saw him as he cradled the game ball the players gave him. "Pop Hog," Theismann exclaimed.

Cooke loved it. So did Bobby Beathard, the Redskins' general manager who was nearby. When he was with the Miami Dolphins they had Larry Csonka, a big back who was quite similar to Riggins.

"John's getting better each week," Beathard smiled. "I just hope we can stay around in the playoffs long enough for him to reach his peak."

By the next evening, the Redskins knew they would play Dallas for the championship. The players had planned on watching the Dallas-Green Bay game on television. To a man, they wanted Dallas. They would be ready. ●

JANUARY 15, 1983
AT RFK STADIUM, WASHINGTON, D.C.
NFC SEMI-FINAL PLAYOFF GAME

Minnesota	0	7	0	0	—	7
Washington	14	7	0	0	—	21

W—Warren, 3 pass from Theismann
   (Moseley kick)
W—Riggins, 2 run (Moseley kick)
M—Brown 18 run (Danmeier kick)
W—Garrett, 18 pass from Theismann
   (Moseley kick)

After completing 17 of 23 passes for 212 yards and a couple of touchdowns, Joe Theismann had plenty of reason to smile.

NFC CHAMPIONSHIP
"I Respect Them
But I Just Don't Like Them"

The war drums began to sound along the banks of the Potomac early Sunday night when Washington and parts of Virginia and Maryland learned that the Dallas Cowboys had defeated the Green Bay Packers 37-26. The Cowboys, the hated Cowboys, would be in Washington the coming Saturday for the NFC Championship. The winner of the conference title would go to Pasadena for the Super Bowl, where each member of the victorious team would receive a booty of $36,000. The Cowboys, the only team that had beaten the Redskins in 11 games, stood in the way of the Super Bowl.

The rivalry between the Cowboys and the Redskins was long lasting. In the past three years, Dallas had won its last six meetings against Washington, including the recent 24-10 triumph in December. In a way, the championship game was a perfect setting. It seemed that destiny had given Washington an opportunity to overcome the final barrier to the Super Bowl. The emotion generated throughout the city was spontaneous. It filled every bar, restaurant, business office and department of government. Washington wasn't the nation's capital but a football-crazed town.

The fervor extended well beyond the 1982 season when Washington had beaten Dallas 26-3 in the title game and made their first and only appearance in a Super Bowl. Even though the Redskins went on to lose Super Bowl VII to Miami, 14-7, it, nevertheless, was the apex of the George Allen era which began in 1971 and lasted through 1977. Ever since, Washington has been a Redskin town; in fact, a one-sport city. The spirit of the Redskins that Allen manifested has prevailed in a city that saw its baseball team leave for Minnesota and its basketball team move to Landover, Maryland. The fans are so loyal that the Redskins have sold out 122 consecutive home games. No other team in the NFL can even approach that figure, not even the Dallas Cowboys, who were baptized "America's Team."

The rivalry is bitter. Art Buchwald, the brilliant satirist whose Washington-based column is syndicated in many newspapers throughout the country, is intense in his dislike for the Cowboys. He has admitted smoking as many as seven cigars during a Dallas contest, not remembering exhaling any of them.

Aaron Latham, a Texas writer living in Washington, who wrote the movie *Urban Cowboy*, is just as disdainful towards the Redskins.

"It's a gut reaction," Latham remarked. "I distrust and dislike government, and that's what the city is all about. I feel most of the country hates Washington, so while I feel out of step with the city, I feel in step with the

Riggins meets a solid Dallas defense as he tightly holds on to the ball.

country."

Actually, the dominating presence of Allen for seven years may have kindled Latham's feelings. Allen and President Richard Nixon were friends who respected one another in their assumption of power. It was Nixon who made Allen head of the nation's physical fitness program. Both attended Whittier College and both played on the football team. Around Dallas, Allen was often referred to as "Richard Nixon with a whistle." While Allen was consumed with football to the point of describing each week's game as Armageddon, Nixon, on the other hand, often talked about world problems in sports language. Nixon's downfall with Watergate, and the accusation of spying by the Cowboys against Allen when he was coach of the Los Angeles Rams, only served to deepen the chasm between Dallas and Washington. A further testament to the paranoia that gripped Allen regarding Dallas was his refusal to call one of his own players, defensive end Dallas Hickman, by his first name.

"George Allen never used to say 'the Dallas Cowboys,'" said John Wilbur, a Redskin guard who played under Allen. "It was always 'the goddamned Dallas Cowboys.' It's the Dallas uniform. It strikes hate and loathing in my mind, almost in a Pavlovian sense."

One has to believe Wilbur. Before joining the Redskins in 1971, he played with the Cowboys from 1966 to 1969. None of the teammates he played with or against remained. The faces might have changed, but the feeling between the teams remained. It is still the Cowboys against the Redskins, and nothing breeds contempt like success.

"In the last few weeks, the fate and fortunes of the Redskins have taken a significant amount of this town's energy," said Fred Wertheimer, head of the Public Affairs Lobby for Common Cause. "Given the fact that the Redskins are winning, and the city is having a tough time, that's not so bad. This town deals with the world's most complex problems daily, and it's nice to get back to basics."

Apparently most of Washington's political figures felt the same way. During the game against Minnesota, the private box of Jack Kent Cooke and Edward Bennett Williams resembled a "Who's Who in the Democratic Party." The guest list included four former presidential candidates: Senator Edward Kennedy, former senators Eugene McCarthy and Edmund Muskie, and Sargent Shriver, Kennedy's brother-in-law. Also included in the group were Joseph Califano, a Washington attorney who served in Jimmy Cart-

Theismann carefully looks to pass. He was careful the entire game, completing 12 of 20 without any interceptions.

143

Kick return specialist Mike Nelms starts to make his move.

er's cabinet and Jack Valenti, a Lyndon Johnson aide who is now director of the Motion Picture Association.

It was against this backdrop of politics and hate, along with the game-day gusto of the rabid Redskin fans, that the biggest event in a decade of Washington sports took place. Getting a ticket was impossible; there weren't any to be had. End zone seats were worth $300 each to scalpers. One enterprising country radio station began playing such songs as "Old Worn Out Cowboys," "Mamas, Don't Let Your Babies Grow Up to

Be Cowboys," and "The Last Cowboy Song." A riot almost occurred on a Washington street when a Redskin fan held up a sign at passing automobiles that read "Honk If You Hate Dallas." Redskin souvenirs were hard to find. Sporting goods stores were nearly sold out of caps, T-shirts and Redskin banners.

Even the politicians were getting involved. The District of Columbia's non-voting congressional delegate, Walter Fauntroy, made a public wager with House Minority Leader Jim Wright, a Texas Democrat, that the losing team's backer would

Dexter Manley put a hit on Dallas quarterback Danny White just before the first half ended that sidelined White the rest of the game.

push the winning team's backer in a wheelbarrow into the House Chamber when Congress went into session the following week.

At a daily White House briefing, deputy press secretary Larry Speakes appeared before the media with a "Beat Dallas" crying towel draped over his lectern. He explained that in the early hours of the morning, an anonymous Redskin fan had placed the towels on the desks of Vice President George Bush and White House chief of staff James Baker, both of whom are Texans.

The enormity of the game even got to Riggins. He hadn't spoken to the press since he came out of retirement for the 1981 season. Now, he wanted to talk. The Redskins marked the occasion by holding a press conference for him. That, too, was big. Eight television stations sent camera crews, and there were more writers than at Nixon's farewell conference.

"I don't have anything cataclysmic to say, except I know you've got some questions stored up," Riggins began. "I would like to say that I'm retiring after Saturday....Just kidding."

He was asked about his request to Gibbs be-

fore the Detroit game that he be given the ball more often.

"It goes back to what I've always said," Riggins answered. "I have to run it 20 times a game at least, or I'm not effective. I told George Allen that one year here. He was halfback-oriented. He said, 'Yeah, okay.' Nothing happened, of course. I build up a rhythm the more I carry it. It takes a while for me to get a feel of how the defense is going to react, who's coming up hard. The good runners can make adjustments on the fly. That's why I don't pay attention to blocking diagrams. I know what's going to happen when I get out there.

"People wonder about the physical toll it takes on me. Well, I feel better at 33 than I did when I was in college, when I could hardly put my feet down in front of each other after a game. Maybe it's because I'm running 35 times instead of running 20 times and blocking at the point of attack the rest of the time. Believe me, that's a lot harder."

"How about the bow you gave the crowd last week?" someone asked.

"What else was I going to do?" Riggins said. "I couldn't high-five them all. Although I'd like to."

"What about the quote you made in 1981 when you came back and said, 'I'm bored, I'm broke, I'm back'?" asked another.

"I don't think I can top that quote," Riggins said. "I may think of something in a minute. But, seriously, that stuff about being bored is certainly true. The hungry football player has an edge. And I came back hungry last year. That's why this game is so important. Look around the league, and you realize how many things have to happen for us to be in this position next year. The young guys are supposed to feel playoff pressure. Well, they shouldn't. They've played in championships of some kind or another ever since they were babies."

Rafael Septien, the Dallas kicker, had sounded like one of those babies after the Green Bay game. Despite kicking three field goals, he apparently was upset that he hadn't received the recognition Moseley did during the season, even though he was six out of six in the playoffs and holds the NFL record for playoff field goals. Of course, he didn't do what Moseley did, kick an NFL record 23 consecutive field goals over two seasons. Septien's remarks only served to light a fire in the Redskin tepee. The Dallas newspapers thought they were inflammatory and didn't print them. However, the Cowboys didn't think much

146

Minutes after Manley's hard tackle, White was still dazed. After receiving treatment from the Dallas trainers, White left the field as the Cowboys huddled with replacement Gary Hogeboom.

of the remarks and included them in a press release.

"He's had a lucky season," Septien said of Moseley. "He's gotten a lot of short ones. Now, he's having problems, and he's probably not ready mentally."

Septien's slur didn't get past a Redskin scout who had been in Dallas observing the game. He changed his flight plans and flew all night to get the release in the hands of a Redskin assistant coach. Naturally, he passed it along to Moseley who had missed three of four field goal attempts in the playoffs.

"There's no need to say something like that," Moseley remarked. "I'm disappointed in Rafael. But we'll settle it on the field Saturday. I'm certainly not happy about my misses but I'm not concerned, either. I'm still knocking the ball good. I'm just miss-hitting it."

Septien's remarks recalled a similar feud between Moseley and the Cowboys several years earlier when Efren Herrera was their kicker. Dallas president Tex Schramm complained that

Moseley's kicking shoe looked illegal, and had league officials check it to see if it was packed with lead.

"One time Herrera hit one from 50 yards, and I hit one from 53, and then he hit a couple more and so did I," Moseley recalled. "Afterward Herrera said, 'Yeah, but I did it without any lead in my shoe.' He didn't have to say that."

Anyone who followed the Redskins knew what Moseley's ability meant to the team's success. He couldn't do anything about Washington's loss to Dallas the first week in December. However, in the game before that and the two that followed, the Washington offense consisted of Moseley. In those three games, against Philadelphia, St. Louis and the New York Giants, the Redskins scored only two touchdowns yet won all three games, simply because Moseley kicked nine field goals.

Although the Redskins were 10-1 and the Cowboys 8-3, the nation's oddsmakers established Dallas as a two-point favorite. Perhaps Washington's critics were placing too much emphasis on the 24-10 loss to Dallas, one in which the Cowboys sacked Theismann seven times and intercepted three of his passes. They also stopped Riggins with only 26 yards on seven carries. Actually, Dallas played the game with the benefit of a ten-day rest. History has shown that Dallas teams traditionally play better in their first post-Thanksgiving game against a less rested opponent. The Redskins had other opinions. They knew they were capable of doing better. ·

"Against the blitz, we just didn't execute very well, but it was a breakdown by the entire unit, not just the line," center Jeff Bostic admitted. "They blitzed a lot more than we expected, and they used a lot of things we didn't anticipate. They came at us with safeties and all such things. Maybe they caught us by surprise. But we are playing better now. We should be able to execute better, and we've seen everything. I don't believe they can catch us again by surprise.

"For us to be successful this time we will have to pound the ball up front with Riggo and keep them from blitzing. If we can get on top early, and John has a good day, we will put a lot of points on the board."

Theismann was the one who had to get them on the board. He appeared confident. He didn't dwell on what happened in the past, but instead drew from experience to benefit him for the week's game.

"Our execution wasn't what it should be, could be or will be," Theismann said. "I think the Cowboys will find we are a different football team this time around. We have a lot more confidence in our capabilities. The team has come together and is playing as well as it can.

"The Cowboys are a great football team, and we will have to play a really good game to win. They came off the ball really well in that first game. I'd imagine they would be doing the same in this one. I think it's a pretty accurate statement to say we haven't done a whole lot against them recently. But I can't think about that last game or any of the other losses to Dallas. What I have to do is look ahead. I know we will have to score more than ten points for us to have a chance to win on Saturday."

Theismann has always played well against the Cowboys. In the last five games against Dallas, he was 78 of 154 for 889 yards. But he had passed for only three touchdowns and had thrown nine interceptions. In the playoffs, Theismann was sharper. He was 31 of 42 for 423 yards, five touchdowns and only one interception. His teammates felt confident.

Danny White, the Cowboy quarterback, had

Dallas defensive tackle John Dutton gives Riggins some rough treatment. Still, Riggins finished the game with 140 yards.

finished second behind Theismann in the NFC rankings. Theismann completed 63.9 percent of his passes, White 63.2. Theismann averaged 8.07 yards per attempt, White 8.42. Theismann accounted for 13 touchdowns and nine interceptions, White 16 touchdowns and 12 interceptions. In the playoffs, White was 50 of 81, 541 yards, three touchdowns and three interceptions. He had the advantage of throwing to two All-Pro wide receivers, Drew Pearson and Tony Hill.

"We know Washington wanted us, and now they have us," White said. "It's going to be the greatest game of the year. They don't like us, and we don't like them. I hope they have 90-foot fences around the field."

Although Riggins had been more effective in the playoffs, the Cowboys still possessed a dangerous runner in Tony Dorsett. As runners, the two are total opposites. Dorsett is a skitterish halfback who has quick acceleration and the moves to go with it. The Washington defense didn't have any trouble with Dorsett the first game, limiting him to just 57 yards in 26 carries. In the two playoff games, Dorsett carried 53 times for 206 yards.

"Right now I feel the third time is the charm," Dorsett said. "We've been beaten the last two times in the championship game, and I'm sitting in my living room, and I hear the chant in Washington that they want Dallas. Well, we're going up there like good doctors. We have a house call to make."

Two hours before the Cowboys were scheduled to arrive on Friday afternoon, the police erected barricades at the entrance of their hotel. Hundreds of Redskin fans had already gathered in the freezing weather, chanting, "We Want Dallas!" The game was still 24 hours away.

"This town has gone crazy," said a local bookmaker. "In the past, you always got Redskin money from some guys who were betting with their hearts. But this time they're convinced they're betting on the better team. There's no doubt in their minds that the Redskins are going to win."

Riggins and the weather were the main areas of concern for Dallas coach Tom Landry. He couldn't do anything about the expected snow. But he hoped to corral Riggins with Dallas' Flex Defense, namely the veteran line of ends Harvey Martin and Too Tall Jones and tackles Randy White and John Dutton, all of whom were strongest at the point of attack.

"If we get a bad day, rain or snow, and the field gets chewed up, that limits your offense," Landry said. "But it's great for a guy like Riggins.

Defensive tackle Darryl Grant's fourth quarter interception, which he ran for a touchdown, clinched Washington's 31-17 victory.

If you let him run on you, you're in trouble. But if you don't let him run, they have to throw the ball. On a heavy field, Riggins will play a very important role. He has played a very important part in their bad-weather games. If Riggins runs well, it will be easier for them to pass. We do like a dry field. We're used to playing on artificial turf."

Gibbs was more used to freewheeling conditions. In only his second season, and a strike-interrupted one at that, he had guided the Redskins to victory in 18 of their last 22 games. His success was so awesome he was named coach of the year. Yet, he remained modest.

"We've had to really struggle to beat people," Gibbs said. "Everybody understands our situation. Dallas has the names. Dallas has the stars. Dallas has the tradition. We have a team with 26 free agents. We have a team of 49 players and very few stars. We've played at our best sometimes and still only won by three points. We're the kind of team that cannot overcome mistakes. We cannot turn the ball over. Dallas can come in

Theismann's 17-yard touchdown pass to Charlie Brown gave the Redskins a 7-3 lead in the first quarter.

151

and make mistakes, they can turn the ball over, and they can overcome those mistakes. They are very talented and very explosive. But for us, things have to go our way.

"The Cowboys go for the big play. They've got people who can do a lot of big things. I just remember that we missed some big plays the first game. We were emotional, but we weren't smooth. In that game they gave us a couple of defensive formations we hadn't seen before. They caused confusion among our blocking backs and confusion in general because Joe had to hang on to the ball a little longer than he's normally used to. We have to do a better job against their blitzing.

"We've been playing very well, but you just have to take it week to week. You never know when it might stop. We just have to continue to be well prepared. I know we feel good about ourselves. There is a confidence factor that carries over from week to week. When players like Joe and John are doing this well, it makes us very consistent. Take Theismann. When he gets in a streak like he's in, he doesn't give up the ball, and he keeps making big passes. And that makes us tough. Most guys in the league, if you give them the ball, 25, 30 times, it takes them two weeks to recover. Not Riggins. Either something's chipped, or cracked or swollen. But John's proven very durable. He can come right back.

"Anytime you play somebody and haven't beaten them, it drives you. If you are competitive, you want to get over that hurdle. I'm sure everybody on the team feels the same way. They are the team that beat us, and you'd like to have that back. This is a chance to play them again."

Gibbs had faced the Cowboys three times and came away empty. That drove him harder during the week. At 42, he found himself in his first championship game against one of the game's coaching legends. Landry, at 58, was in his tenth championship contest in 13 years. His teams have missed the playoffs only once in 17 years. Gibbs didn't feel overwhelmed at all.

"I don't know Tom Landry, except to say hello, perhaps," Gibbs said. "We've never talked about football, never had any discussion. Respect him? Of course. But I can't regard this as a coaches' game. I never think about the other coach. I just think about the game, how we play it, and how they play it."

Like the Redskins, the Cowboys use a lot of motion. They try to confuse their opponents with finesse and misdirection plays. Most experts had predicted that the NFC title game would come to Washington. Yet, the prognosis was that the Cowboys would win as they had done so many times before. The Redskin players weren't buying it. They were still looking for the respect that was denied them all season long. They knew a victory over the Cowboys would get them it.

"I respect them but I just don't like them," said Manley, who wore an "I Hate Dallas!" cap at practice. "Even if they beat us, they are going to pay the price in RFK. The only reason I don't like them is that I'm here, in Washington. How can I live here, in this town, and say I like the Dallas Cowboys? Besides, we need to win this game to get the respect we deserve. People should be convinced by now, but if we get to the Super Bowl, they'll have to think we're good."

Theismann shared the same feelings. "I think fans across the country, and the national media, are starting to sit up and notice that the Redskins are pretty special," he said.

It was up to Theismann to keep it that way. He needed a big game, and got a good day for it. It didn't rain or snow. Instead, the day was cloudy and 38 degrees. Everyone who had a ticket showed up; 55,045 seats were filled. All that remained was the game. Nothing more could be said or done.

The Cowboys had their opportunity to score first. They won the coin toss and put the ball in play on the 15-yard line following Jeff Hayes' kick to the goal line. Dorsett tested the Washington defense and got three yards. White then timed a sideline pattern to Pearson who caught the ball and immediately stepped out of bounds on the 26. It was a first down. Ron Springs, Dallas' other running back, found a hole and moved for 12 yards before he was brought down on the 38. After Dorsett got three more yards, White threw a 14-yard pass to Hill, his other wide receiver. The Cowboys had another first down on the Washington 45 and were moving smoothly. Mark Murphy then made his third straight tackle by stopping Springs after he gained three yards. White went back to Pearson and completed a 14-yard pass on the 28. Dorsett got a yard and then five before White hooked up with his tight end Doug Cosbie on the 15-yard line. It was Dallas' fifth first down and Redskin fans were nervous.

They cheered when Manley dropped Springs for no gain. They cheered again when Dorsett fumbled on the next play only to find disappointment when Cosbie recovered the ball on the ten. Washington's defense faced the challenge of not only stopping a first down but also the possibility of a touchdown. Cornerback Vernon Dean

Riggins quietly celebrates after the game by having a few beers with friends in the RFK Stadium parking lot.

Darryl Grant makes sure he catches Dallas quarterback Gary Hogeboom's pass that was deflected by Dexter Manley. Grant ran ten yards for the game's final touchdown.

played Pearson close and prevented him from catching White's third down pass. It meant that Septien, who was booed by the Redskin fans when he appeared, would try a 27-yard field goal. He was successful, and the Cowboys jumped into a 3-0 lead. They had done so by going 75 yards on 14 plays and using almost eight minutes of the clock.

The Redskins' first offensive series began on the 16-yard line. Not unexpectedly, Riggins ran on the first play and got seven yards. He carried again and gained five to the 28 and a first down. Theismann threw his first pass and completed it to his right end Rick Walker for nine yards. It was time for Riggins again. He got the first down by gaining three yards to the 40. Theismann then got the Redskins into Dallas' territory with a 15-yard pass to his other tight end Don Warren. Redskin fans felt something good happening as Washington reached the Dallas 45. Theismann was mixing his plays well.

On an end around, Riggins handed the ball to Garrett, but the Cowboys were ready and linebacker Bob Breunig dropped Garrett for a two-

yard loss. Undaunted, Theismann came back to Garrett and completed an 11-yard pass on the Dallas 36. On third and one, the situation was made for Riggins. He didn't disappoint. Rather, he shook the Cowboys by breaking loose for 17 yards to the 19. Redskin fans cheered loudly. Theismann asked for quiet as he prepared to take the snap. Then, he, too, stunned the Cowboys. He sent wide receiver Charlie Brown out on a quick fly pattern and hit him perfectly with a 19-yard touchdown pass. Dallas couldn't believe it. Moseley was perfect on the conversion to send the Redskins into a 7-3 lead.

Rod Hill gave the Redskins some anxious moments with his kickoff return. He broke clear of the pack, and it appeared he might go all the way until Hayes knocked him out of bounds on the Dallas 35-yard line. White then proceeded to hit Hill with an eight-yard pass on the 43. Manley came up with another big play when he dumped Dorsett for a yard loss. On third down, White decided to throw but his pass was incomplete. Punting for the first time, White's kick wasn't very long. It only covered 31 yards, and Mike Nelms'

13-yard return gave the Redskins an advantageous field position on their own 40.

Only one play remained before the first period came to a close. Riggins made it a big one. He cracked the Dallas defense for 11 yards. On five carries in the opening period, Riggins had already produced 43 yards. He began the second period by running for six more. Theismann kept giving Riggins the ball. He got two yards and then another. On fourth and one on the 40, Washington decided to go for it. It was Riggins again, and he made it to the 39 for the first down.

Theismann then switched to a pass play but threw incomplete. After Joe Washington couldn't gain anything, Theismann came through with a 22-yard completion to Garrett and a first down on the 17-yard line. Washington was threatening again. Riggins moved forward for two yards to the 15. However, on the next play, the Redskins were penalized for having an illegal receiver downfield. The ten-yard penalty placed the ball back on the 25-yard line. Theismann had to pass now. He threw to Garrett for eight yards on the 17. Nick Giaquinto replaced Riggins and immediately got involved in the action. He was held up by cornerback Dennis Thurman, as he tried to get open in the Dallas secondary. The penalty was costly. It gave the Redskins a first down on the 12-yard line.

Riggins returned to the lineup and picked up two yards. The crowd was urging the Redskins on for a touchdown. Theismann tried. He threw a pass to Walker that was knocked away by Randy White. On third down he looked for Warren but failed to reach him with his pass. Moseley trotted onto the field to the encouragement of the Redskin fans, who were upset by Septien's pregame remarks. Theismann marked the spot for a 27-yard field goal. The ball got off but was erred in its flight. Moseley's slump continued.

Washington's defense continued to play tough. After White threw a nine-yard pass to tight end Billy Joe DuPree, they rejected Dallas' attempt for a first down. First Butz stopped Springs at the line of scrimmage, and then safety Tony Peters came up and tackled Dorsett for no gain. White had to punt and again he experienced difficulty. His kick only went 29 yards, landing out of bounds on the Redskin 42.

For the second straight time, the Redskins had excellent attack position. Riggins began with a two-yard gain. Theismann still had trouble passing. He threw without success to Brown and then to Garrett. It was the fourth interception in a row. Hayes then got off a 45-yard punt that Hill waited

for on the 11-yard line. He never caught it. Instead, he fumbled and reserve linebacker Monte Coleman pounced on the ball so quickly that for a moment nobody knew who he was. He was indeed the newest hero.

The Redskins couldn't miss this opportunity to score. Safety Benny Barnes had to bring down Riggins after he got five yards. Riggins carried again and gained three yards to the three-yard line. While everyone was expecting Riggins, it was Washington who ran to the one-yard line and a first down. Theismann quieted the crowd again. Now everybody watched Riggins. He took Theismann's handoff and dove into the end zone for a touchdown. Moseley converted and stretched Washington's advantage to 14-3.

For the third time, the Cowboys failed to produce a first down. White tried three passes and missed on all of them. When his punt only went 33 yards, the Redskins were again presented with an even better field position on their own 48-yard line. With 2:08 left in the first half, they had time to score. Theismann tried to make it happen but was sacked for a nine-yard loss by White. After he threw incomplete to Washington, he came right back to the little halfback for a 13-yard completion on the Dallas 48. The Redskins were still six yards short of a first down, and Hayes punted into the Dallas end zone.

Only 1:57 remained when Dallas started the action on the 20-yard line. White came out throwing. His first pass was negated by a motion penalty that set the Cowboys back to the 15. Avoiding the rush, White hit Dorsett with a quick pass that carried to the 40-yard line. Only 39 seconds remained when the Cowboys called time out. When the game resumed, White connected with his other back, Robert Newhouse, for a 16-yard gain on the Washington 40 before he went out of bounds. Throwing again, White passed 12 yards to wide receiver Butch Johnson. Dallas called time with 31 seconds to go.

The Cowboys wanted to score before the half ended. White dropped to pass again. Manley charged him and knocked him to the ground just as he threw the ball. The pass fell untouched on the ground as White lay still, seemingly knocked out from the force of Manley's blow. White had to leave the game and was replaced by Gary Hogeboom who had thrown only eight passes in the three years he had been with the Cowboys. Before the first half ended, Hogeboom managed to complete a nine-yard pass to running back Timmy Newsome. The Redskins left the field ahead, 14-3, encouraged by the cheers of the noisy crowd.

White appeared dazed while making his way to the Dallas dressing room. If the Cowboys hoped to overtake the Redskins with a second-half rally, they would need him. During the halftime respite, doctors attended White and X-rays were taken to determine the extent of his injury. The final analysis was that he had suffered a concussion and could not play anymore that day. He returned to the Dallas bench after the half, bowed his head and tried to hold back the tears. If the Cowboys were going to win, it would not be with White, but with an inexperienced quarterback from Central Michigan University, Gary Hogeboom.

Washington didn't do anything after receiving the second-half kickoff. Nelms fumbled, and Giaquinto alertly recovered the ball on the seven-yard line. After Riggins moved the ball out to the ten, Theismann failed to complete two passes. Hayes' punt carried only to the Washington 43-yard line and a five-yard runback placed the ball on the 38.

Appearing poised and confident, Hogeboom began throwing as if he had been doing it all season. First, he completed a 15-yard pass to Hill on the 23. After an incomplete pass, and one to Newsome that lost a yard, Hogeboom hit Johnson with a 15-yard pass and a first down on the nine. Dorsett got the Cowboys closer to a touchdown by getting to the six. On the next play Hogeboom got it. He drilled a touchdown pass to Pearson in the corner of the end zone. Septien kicked the extra point, and the Cowboys closed to within 14-10.

On the kickoff, Mike Nelms brought the crowd to its feet. He took Septien's kick on the four and began one of his patented runbacks. He cut past a couple of Dallas tacklers and broke free along the sidelines. Only a desperate tackle by Thurman on the Dallas 20 prevented Nelms from scoring a touchdown. The Redskins had an excellent scoring opportunity. Theismann handed to Riggins who got only a yard. Playing pass, Dallas blitzed two linebackers and nailed Theismann for a nine-yard sack back on the 28. It didn't bother Theismann. On third and long he threw a 22-yard pass to Brown on the Dallas six-yard line. Theismann wanted Riggins at this point. He got two yards to the four. Again Riggins, and this time he powered his way into the end zone. Moseley converted and Washington increased its lead to 21-10.

Dallas didn't quit. Following the kickoff, the brassy Hogeboom led the Cowboys on an 84-yard drive and a touchdown, converting four

third down situations in the process. Dorsett began the drive with a three-yard gain. After an incompleted pass, Hogeboom completed one to Butch Johnson and a first down on the 29. Dorsett then took off on his longest run of the game, getting 17 yards to the 46. Hogeboom missed with a pass but Dorsett got eight more yards on a run and four on a pass for another first down on the Washington 42. Then Hogeboom hit Hill for 12 yards on the 30. Following two incompleted passes, Hogeboom kept the drive going with a ten-yard completion to Hill on the 20. Dorsett got to the 17. However, the Cowboys lost six yards when they tried an end around with Hill carrying. On third and 13, Hogeboom came through with a big play. He fired a 23-yard touchdown pass to Johnson. Septien's extra point narrowed the gap once again, 21-17.

There was 3:25 remaining in the third period when Washington went on the offense. However, they couldn't accomplish much. Riggins was stopped for no gain. A defensive holding penalty managed to give the Redskins a first down on the 22-yard line. Then Theismann was sacked again, this time for a nine-yard loss on the 13. Although he completed a nine-yard pass to Warren and a four-yard one to Harmon, the Redskins had to punt.

Only 14 seconds were left when the Cowboys opened up with good field position on their 45-yard line. Hogeboom threw quickly. After missing his first two passes, he connected with Pearson on the last play of the third quarter, an 11-yard completion on the Washington 44. When Hogeboom hit Cosbie with a 19-yard pass to begin the fourth period, the Cowboys appeared to be coming back. Dorsett then got down to the 20-yard line with a five-yard run. Running again, he lost three yards when Peters came up quickly from his safety spot. On third down, Hogeboom had to pass, but he threw low after being rushed. Septien came in to try a 42-yard field goal but his kick sailed wide, much to the delight of the crowd.

Again Washington's offense bogged down. A Theismann to Garrett pass gained five yards, and then Riggins ran for four; but, on third down, needing only a yard, Riggins was stopped. Washington had to punt. They needed a big play from the defense to halt Dallas' momentum. The Redskins got it on the first play. Hogeboom tried to pass to Hill but linebacker Mel Kaufman read the play beautifully and intercepted on the Dallas 40. Washington had to make the most of the turnover. A four point lead with 10:40 left wasn't

Manley did in Danny White and the Cowboys with this hard hit shortly before the first half action ended.

enough. Riggins ran for four yards and then picked up another. On third down, Theismann and Brown combined on a 13-yard pass on the 21. The strategy was to use Riggins. He ran for three yards, then five and finally one more. The Redskins were still one yard short of a first down on the 12. On fourth and one, Moseley was sent in to kick a 29-yard field goal. He felt the pressure but, nevertheless, kicked the ball perfectly to give Washington a 24-17 lead.

The game clock flashed 7:12 when Dallas put the ball in play on the 20-yard line following the kickoff. Hogeboom dropped back to pass. He was trying to set up a delayed screen to his left. Manley charged him. Hogeboom tried to throw while still fading back. Manley tipped the ball high into the air, and Grant, coming from the outside, caught it. There wasn't anybody in front of him as he ran for a touchdown. The Redskin defense had forced another turnover. Washington fans were ready to celebrate as Moseley's conversion sent the Redskins into a 31-17 lead.

Dallas' only hope was to score quickly. Time was the Cowboys' enemy now. There wasn't anything else to do but pass. Hogeboom got 16 yards on a completion to Pearson on the 44-yard line. After an incompletion, Dorsett tried to cross

up the Washington defense by breaking off a long run; he was stopped after five yards. When Hogeboom connected with Johnson for 13 yards, Dallas had a first down on the Washington 38. Five minutes remained. Washington braced for the Dallas air assault. The Redskin defense was marvelous. Four times Hogeboom fired, and each time he was repelled.

It was practically over. Washington was only 4:26 away from their first championship in a decade. The Redskins took over on their 38-yard line with but a single mission, kill the clock. That was left to Riggins. He ran and he ran: two yards, eight yards, four yards and then 12 more yards. Dallas called time. Riggins got five and Dallas called time again. It gave Riggins a breather. He came back with six yards and one yard and three more for another first down. Dallas asked that the clock be stopped for a third time. It was useless. It only prolonged the agony of defeat. The crowd began singing "Hail to the Redskins." Riggins added two more yards after carrying the ball an unbelievable nine straight times. To the appreciation of the fans, he left the field with 44 seconds remaining. Theismann then took the final snap and went down on one knee. He got up and carried the ball to the Redskin bench where he was

157

Redskin players carry Joe Gibbs off the field following 34-17 victory over Dallas.

embraced by his teammates. Washington fans rushed onto the field. The Redskins were champions. They were going to Pasadena. Hail to the Redskins, indeed.

However, it wasn't over. The officials indicated that there were still 12 seconds officially left to play. In a bizarre setting, they made the Cowboys and Redskins leave their dressing rooms and return to the field as the public address announcer pleaded with the fans to leave the gridiron. It was a charade. Wide receiver Drew Pearson took the snap from the center and killed the ball. Now it was official. The Redskins were kings. Redskin fans heralded the occasion by chanting "We Beat Dallas." Nothing could be sweeter. The

Washington players carried Gibbs off the field on their shouldders.

The Redskin dressing room was bedlam. Dave Butz had a cigar in his mouth, and so did practically every other player. Butz had saved a box for this occasion, and he handed them out to his teammates. Owners Jack Kent Cooke and Edward Bennett Williams were there, as was Bobby Beathard and dozens of other well wishers. Joe Blair, the club's veteran public relations director, had all he could do to maintain some semblance of order in a sea of hysteria. He had to secure some of the game's stars for live television interviews.

What took precedence above all else, however, was a telephone call from President Reagan who had watched the game from the presidential retreat in Camp David. Gibbs took the phone call.

"I just want to congratulate you and all that great gang of yours," Reagan began. "What an afternoon this has been. Well, listen, I just wanted to say if the fellows feel like, when the season is over, letting down easy, I could use them helping me up there with Congress."

Gibbs smiled. "This has been a team effort here, as you know. Everybody in Washington deserves the credit. Everybody."

The brief phone call ended and Gibbs expounded more upon what it all meant.

"You are witnessing the happiest moment in someone's life right now," Gibbs said. "The first time I really talked about the Super Bowl to our guys was just before this game. I told them history was providing us a thumbnail sketch of the coming Super Bowl champions, and we had an opportunity to do something about it. We put everything we had into this game, but I don't see that affecting us in the Super Bowl because this group has been able to keep the proper frame of mind. All this was the whole world rolled into one game. This was the way it was supposed to be, the Redskins vs. Dallas, in RFK, for the NFC title, with the Super Bowl at stake. How can you top that?

"Riggins has been super. On game days, John tells us, 'Hey, just get the wagon out, hitch it up, and I'll pull it. Everybody get on it.'"

Riggins was pulling the wagon west, to California. He had run with amazing success. In still another record-shattering performance, he carried the ball 36 times for 140 yards. In the final period he ran with the ball a staggering 16 times and collected 62 yards. Big, 33-year-old fullbacks aren't supposed to do that. In three playoff games he gained 444 yards in comparison with the eight regular season games where he had 553.

"I waited a long time for this," Riggins said. "I'm really thrilled. To tell you the truth, after the strike I was ready to pack my bags and head home for Kansas. Boy, what a mistake that would have been."

Riggins' buddy, guard Russ Grimm, explained why Riggins was much more effective this time against Dallas.

"We changed so much stuff for this game," Grimm revealed. "Last time we zone-blocked. This time we went more man-to-man, more double teams. We decided to take them on, be physical, let the best man win."

As far as Theismann was concerned, the Redskins were the best. They proved it today.

"We don't care, we really don't care what other people say about us," Theismann said. "They say we're lucky, that we don't have enough talent to win. Well, whatever it is, we've done it. I'll let the facts speak for themselves. We started the season the same as everyone else, and we made it all the way. If we're a fluke, you can just put NFC champion right behind it.

"On this team, and this is the closest team I've been on in nine years, no one player is greater than any other. When we get our opportunities, we do make the most of them. They have done it all season. Anyone who still wonders whether this gritty band of Redskins is for real has been living under a rock.

"This is the happiest moment of my life. The kids I love to death, but I can't imagine being any happier than I am right now. Playing in the Super Bowl is like a dream come true. You want to do something so bad for so long, and all of a sudden it becomes a reality. I want to jump up and scream and yell. I'll probably cry like a baby."

If anyone wanted to cry from exhaustion, it could very easily have been Manley or Grant, for that matter. Manley's hit had sent White to the sidelines for the rest of the game, and his deflection of Hogeboom's pass enabled Grant to score the clinching touchdown in the fourth period.

"Can I rest a while?" Manley asked while still in his uniform 90 minutes after the game ended. "It was a very emotional game for Dexter Manley. I hit White head-on with a good shot. I felt bad when I saw he was having trouble getting up, because I never want to hurt anyone. With White out, I thought we had the advantage because I never heard of the other guy. But the Cowboys came out in the second half really motivated. I

was honestly getting mad because Dallas was moving the football. My teammates had to calm me down on the sidelines. Somebody had to take charge, so I did."

He did so on that one play that resulted in Grant's interception.

"I felt it was a screen right away," Grant said. "You battle a guy hard all day and all of a sudden he slides off you and you get into the backfield awfully quick. It's not too hard to read a screen when that happens. All I was doing was trying to get into the middle of the play. I was more concerned with the receiver not pulling down the ball and making a long gain than anything else.

"I was kind of dizzy following the ball. I had to twist around and get myself oriented. I wasn't sure about catching it at all. First I thought, 'Hey, you can catch that ball.' Then I just ran as hard as I could. It didn't hit me that I actually scored until everyone started pounding me. Then I thought, 'Wow, I scored.' Then I just remember being tired from all that piling on."

If no one respected the Redskins by now, it was certain the Cowboys did. Last year Dallas was angry because they felt they had let the game get away from them against San Francisco. This time they were beaten. It didn't take much to see why.

"We were playing for the Super Bowl," Drew Pearson said in the Dallas dressing room. "The Redskins were playing for respect. They got both."

That's all they ever wanted. But the season wasn't over yet.   ●

JANUARY 22, 1983
AT RFK STADIUM, WASHINGTON, D.C.
NFC CHAMPIONSHIP GAME

Washington	7	7	7	10 —	31
Dallas	3	0	14	0 —	17

D—FG, Septien, 27
W—Brown, 17 pass from Theismann (Moseley kick)
W—Riggins 1 run (Moseley kick)
D—Pearson, 6 pass from Hogeboom (Septien kick)
W—Riggins 4 run (Moseley kick)
D—Johnson, 23 pass from Hogeboom (Septien kick)
W—FG, Moseley, 29
W—Grant 10 interception return (Moseley kick)

SUPER BOWL XVII
"Beating Dallas Was Super Bowl One; Now We Play Super Bowl Two"

The emotional trauma of the Redskins' victory over the Cowboys had ramifications that reached far from the playing field. Capitol Hill was in a turmoil. The Republicans and Democrats were at odds over President Reagan's budget. The President pleaded for cooperation, but with no success.

Yet, whether Republican or Democrat, one could sense that the Redskins' magnificent triumph was causing the legislators to put aside their political differences. Some were playfully self-indulgent. Senator John Warner of Virginia made a bet with Senator Paula Hawkins of Florida. They used the steps of the Capitol to stage their prank. If the Redskins lost, Warner would wear a Miami Dolphin jersey, while Hawkins would don a Redskin jersey if Miami lost. Eugene McCarthy, former senator from Minnesota, hailed the Redskin victory as monumental. He made the following observations in a *New York Times* article:

> "It was as though Gabriel had blown the last trumpet and all had been saved. There could scarcely be any greater natural public joy than that which ran through the hearts and minds of the residents of Washington following the Redskins' victory over the Dallas Cowboys...
>
> "What may happen in the Super Bowl against some team mildly called the Dolphins is of secondary, if any, importance...
>
> "Washington has a thing about Dallas. Any presidential candidate can go to Dallas, denounce Washington and be wildly approved. In the political order of the United States, Dallas has become to Washington what Constantinople was to Rome in the earlier age of faith. Now Washington has prevailed over Dallas, the Redskins have beaten the Cowboys, an achievement sustained by the scriptural promise that 'the mighty will be brought down and those who have been humiliated, exalted.' And then the final scriptural justification, 'Let us rejoice and be glad,' which is what Washingtonians were and still are."

After such a stunning victory, Gibbs, as usual, kept things in perspective. He did not let euphoria overcome his team's long preparation for the Super Bowl. He allowed his players a night of celebration after Saturday's charismatic victory over the Cowboys. On Sunday, he gave them a day off enabling them not only to see the New York Jets-Miami AFC championship game but to size up their opponent the following Sunday in Pasadena. Meanwhile, Gibbs and his staff used Sunday to work at the Redskins' training compound near Dulles Airport. The players were allowed to work out if they wished to; but most of them opted to look at the team they would be playing in Super Bowl XVII.

The Washington defense puts the squeeze on Miami running back Tony Nathan.

Although Gibbs is a self-admitted workaholic, he didn't insist on working on the Sunday after a game. In a normal season, there is a two-week span between the conference championships and the Super Bowl game. Since the season was shortened by the unprecedented players' strike which reduced the regular campaign to nine games, the playoffs were extended, and the normal open weekend before the Super Bowl game was utilized to determine the NFC and AFC championships. Gibbs and general manager Bobby Beathard had to make quick decisions on the team's final travel plans to the West Coast. They had an extra day, unlike the Dolphins who began finalizing their itinerary long into Sunday night, having disposed of the Jets 14-0.

Both teams were expected by league mandate to arrive in Los Angeles by Monday evening. The Redskins, designated as the home team, were staying at the South Coast Plaza Hotel in Costa Mesa. They had an additional advantage in being able to use the Los Angeles Rams' training facilities, which were not only close by but designed to pro standards. The Dolphins were billetted at the Marriott in Newport Beach and had use of the training field of Fullerton State College. The arrangements for both teams had been determined two weeks earlier when representatives of the four final playoff teams had met with league officials in Los Angeles and were shown the practice facilities that were considered acceptable. After a photo session scheduled for both teams at their respective training sites on Tuesday, the clubs were to begin serious workouts for their Sunday confrontation in the picturesque Rose Bowl.

The preparation took place during inclement weather. A snarling Pacific storm approached the shores of southern California, and high seas and heavy rains were expected. After a partly sunny afternoon, which satisfied the photographers, the rain began to fall. It created havoc to the south of Los Angeles. Santa Monica and Redondo Beach experienced extensive property damage from wind, and high tides created such calamity by the week's end that the area was eligible for federal aid.

By Friday the unseasonal rain and a second storm warning made a ticket to the game in the open Rose Bowl less desirable. In California, over-charging for tickets is legal, and the many ticket agencies in Los Angeles had expected a bonanza. They had priced 40-yard line seats as high as $400 and were asking $150 for end zone locations normally priced at $40. Their big dollar margin began to diminish with each day of rain, and many of the astute brokers were faced with the fear of being stuck with tickets. Some planned to dispose of the tickets at face value on Sunday morning, well before the 3 p.m. kickoff. It was a drastic contrast to last year's game in Pontiac, Michigan. Murray's Tickets and Travel had sold 8,000 tickets to that game. This time, the game was local, and the agency didn't expect to sell more than 3,500 tickets.

The weather notwithstanding, Los Angeles entrepreneurs had hoped for a Dallas-New York Super Bowl. Ticket brokers felt that they could easily get $500 a ticket for that match-up. Washington versus Miami wasn't the same. Hotel executives anticipated bigger profits if Dallas had won simply because they concluded that the Cowboys had a larger fan following, one that spends more money. In fact, the Biltmore Hotel was so convinced that the Cowboys would defeat the Redskins in the NFC championship that they launched an advertising campaign in the Dallas area two weeks before the Super Bowl. The results were encouraging. However, when the Redskins emerged victorious, the hotel received a flood of telephone calls canceling reservations. After reaching the Super Bowl with the best record in the NFL, Washington still hadn't received the respect such an accomplishment should merit.

"We're basically an unknown team," said linebacker Rich Milot. "A lot of people underestimated us."

Gibbs preferred it that way. What he had to worry about was his own players' happiness at just being in the Super Bowl. Teams that talk and feel that way often end up with the loser's purse, which this year was a record $25,000. Since the Redskins had beaten their most hated rival, the Cowboys, only 48 hours before, Gibbs had to make certain his players hadn't peaked emotionally. He recognized such a possibility just after the Redskins arrived in Los Angeles. Tackle Lou Jacoby couldn't contain his delight in defeating Dallas.

"This was our Super Bowl," he remarked.

Like most of his teammates who expressed the same sentiments, Jacoby is young. However, his joy in beating Dallas had to be placed in perspective. It took veteran tackle George Starke to do just that.

"Beating Dallas was Super Bowl One," corrected Starke quickly before any other players could get carried away with Jacoby's outlook. "Now we play Super Bowl Two."

Riggins surprised everyone at owner Jack Kent Cooke's pre-Super Bowl party by attending affair in top hat and tails. He takes a moment to clown with columnist Carl Rowan.

162

"Ah," added center Jeff Bostic, "nothing seems to bother us."

Still, Gibbs had to make sure. "No question, coming off a big win over Dallas could be a problem," he said. "Our game with Dallas was everything rolled into one. We had not beaten them since I've been in Washington, and Dallas gave us our only loss of the season this year. If you're a Redskin fan, you don't like Dallas. The Dallas game wasn't like Miami beating the Jets. Miami beat the Jets twice this year. We hadn't beaten Dallas, period. We lost to them three straight times since I've been here, and it was something we had to have. We played as well as we could. I think the players will turn right around and adjust to playing in the Super Bowl. This team is unusual in that it gave a high-level performance all year. Even in the Dallas game we lost, we laid it out there.

"I don't believe things happen by accident. I think somebody is in charge of the world. I don't believe in two amoebas hitting the same puddle, and we end up here today with man and woman. As far as football, things happen for a reason. Whether we're destined to win the thing or not, I don't know. But I think we were supposed to play last week in the championship game. It wasn't supposed to be anybody else. They were the one team that beat us this year. We were undefeated with the exception of Dallas. It stuck in our craw. We wanted to eliminate that. We didn't want to go past the NFC game if it was anybody else but Dallas.

"We're a championship team. We know what's at stake. This is a chance to attain something we may never have an opportunity to get again. We cannot have the excuse that we left our game on the field last week. This is an opportunity we can't blow. If we blow this, if we walk away from here and lose this game, most people won't be able to recall who Miami beat. Maybe that's not right, but it's a fact. That's the nature of the business.

"We know that Miami is the favorite. We know we're going in as underdogs. I don't know if it is an advantage, but it's something we have had to live with all season. We let others evaluate whether we should have respect now or not. We just play. It's just that we have to do everything right. We can't afford to turn the ball over. We're not the kind of talented team that can come back from two or three touchdowns and catch people. We've been that way all year. We're just not a dominating kind of football team. We're going to lay everything we have out on the field. If we beat Miami, we deserve the gold ring."

Guard Russ Grimm was determined to open holes for Riggins when the second half began.

There was a tinge of *déjà vu* involving the game, more so for Miami coach Don Shula than anyone else. This was Shula's fifth appearance in the Super Bowl. Only Dallas coach Tom Landry had participated in as many. Yet, the one that Shula remembers most was Super Bowl VII in 1973. It was the first one he won when the Dolphins completed an undefeated 17-game season with a 14-7 victory over the Redskins. The game that year was also played in Los Angeles, only at The Coliseum. In fact, it was the last Super Bowl game played there as Super Bowl XI and XIV were both fought at the more spacious Rose Bowl. In the 1972 NFC championship game, the Redskins also had to get past Dallas. It was Washington's first championship in 30 years; and Starke, a member of the taxi squad that season, was the only player on the 1982 team who had any previous Super Bowl exposure.

Starke, who was classified as injured reserve at the time, never forgot the Redskins' previous Super Bowl experience. Coach George Allen had worked himself almost into a state of paranoia before the Redskins ever got to Los Angeles. He worried about the distractions his players would be subjected to from the media. He was con-

Riggins was the Redskin workhorse all afternoon. He carried the ball 38 times for an amazing 166 yards, both new Super Bowl records.

165

EXPLODE

This pass play that Coach Joe Gibbs put in especially for the Super Bowl resulted in two touchdown passes from quarterback Joe Theismann to wide receiver Charlie Brown.

cerned about security and changed hotels to alleviate both pitfalls. At the Saddleback Inn in Santa Ana, Allen cordoned his players and coaches in one wing, allowing nobody from outside to even walk in the corridors. To maximize security, Allen hired a former Long Beach policeman to patrol the halls. It was a tight atmosphere indeed. He imposed a curfew every night; and his players, who were mostly veteran campaigners, resented the sanctions.

"That was a mistake," Starke said. "The Dolphins were having a good time, and the rest of us were real tight. That's why Miami won the game. I think Joe Gibbs is taking a much more reasonable approach. Allen spent so much time worrying about distractions that he created a lot of them that weren't there. Football is football; and although this week is different from normal, he made the distractions a bigger issue than they had to be.

"We're practicing at the Rams' facility, and there is no way that George Allen would ever have us practice there. There are open fences and an apartment complex on one side of the field. That would have driven him crazy because he's paranoid about being secretive. George would have had to rent the entire apartment building."

It was a lot different back then. George Allen was the coach with his "future is now" philosophy and Richard Nixon was the President. Nixon didn't hide his love for the Redskins. Although he wasn't known for any football prowess

during his college days at Whittier, Nixon, nevertheless, became somewhat of an observing expert. He volunteered to help his beloved Redskins in the Super Bowl game against Miami. He diagrammed a play which Allen thanked him for but never used.

Although Allen was Nixon's favorite, he was far from such with defensive tackle Dave Butz, who was signed by Allen as a free agent in 1975. Butz shudders to think what the atmosphere might be if Allen were still the coach.

"George's deal was to use only the veterans every down of every game from the start of the season to the end," Butz explained. "Even when we were ahead by 20 points, he stayed with the veterans when he should have been giving the younger guys some experience. As a result, when the playoffs came, the veterans were burned out.

"George's other thing was game preparation. Football, football, and nothing but football. If he was coaching us now, he would have secluded us from the press and kept us away from anything but football. Gibbs is much different. He treats us like adults. Before we came out here, he told us just one thing—don't do anything that hurts the team. As long as we stay aware of that rule, we're okay. He's left us on our own after 5 o'clock each afternoon until the next morning. He told us to be in by midnight. If we wanted to stay up a little later than that, fine, but just stay in your hotel room. There won't be any bed checks on this team."

That was fine with Riggins. Although he was a

Miami coach Don Shula has a worried look in the second half.

marked man, he was loose. In the past month he was running better than he ever had in his career, which gave him a sense of accomplishment and inner satisfaction regarding his performance in contributing heavily to the team's success. He had run through the playoffs like a man possessed, gaining an almost unbelievable 444 yards in 98 carries. No wonder Riggins was loose. He was on a roll. When an athlete is in such a groove, he is unflappable. Riggins was always one to march to the beat of his own drummer, and now the drum was beating ever so loudly. But at the photo day assemblage, Riggins appeared numb. He stared forlornly at the southern California horizon, perhaps daydreaming about the plains of Kansas, not paying much attention to the questions being asked him. The next day he attended the first press session with the rest of his teammates. In a crowded room of reporters, Riggins not only stood behind a microphone for an individual press conference, but he did so with a flourish, dressed in camouflage pants with an elephant-gun belt buckle protruding from his waist.

However, Riggins saved his best escapades for nightfall. He and several teammates, including guard Russ Grimm, decided it was party time, and party they did on Wednesday. They returned to the hotel at around 3 a.m., feeling frivolous, and woke up their sleeping teammates. Grimm admitted that they had had a few here and there at several bars. He said nobody was inebriated; but nevertheless, the party-goers did have a "buzz" on.

Friday night was something else. Riggins was invited to another party, only this time an acceptable one. Owner Jack Kent Cooke hosted a private party for his beloved players. It was specified as a strictly informal affair. What did Riggins do? He turned out in white tie, white gloves, top hat, and tails. His resplendent appearance so enthralled the guests that he was accorded a standing ovation. Riggins was loose indeed.

In reality, he had to be. There was no doubt that he was the hunted. All week long, coaches, analysts, reporters, even some knowledgeable fans chanted the same refrain: "Stop Riggins and you can stop the Redskins." Yet, it was the kind of challenge that Riggins loved. He wasn't the least bit fazed by all the pre-game analysts centered around him or how much he would be called upon to carry the ball in various operations.

"Those plays never seem to work the way they do on the blackboard," Riggins said. "The de-

Charlie Brown looks for running room against Dolphins after catching a pass from Theismann.

fense has an idea how they want to stop the plays, too. The better ball carriers, the ones who stay around a while, can read the defense. You have to find the daylight."

If anything, Riggins stood out in the daylight. He is the lone runner in Washington's one-back formation behind quarterback Joe Theismann. Riggins had to run against a Miami defense that employed a 3-4 alignment, three down linemen and four linebackers. Yet, it wasn't a defense that Riggins or the rest of the offensive players weren't familiar with. Miami's defensive scheme was supposed to give the quarterback a wide variety of looks and create disruption of the offense's blocking techniques. Gibbs wasn't the least bit perturbed. He openly explained the use of his one-back formation.

"The four-receiver concept fits our personnel very well," Gibbs pointed out. "If we played two backs simultaneously, one would have to do the blocking for the other. When Riggins carried, Joe Washington, who weighs only 180 pounds, would have to block for him. We would rather have one of those blocks sitting on the bench

Center Jeff Bostic: "We wanted to make John very tough running the ball."

resting and have a 250-pound tight end blocking for us.

"Second, our offense is better suited to the widespread use of the 3-4 defense. In our original schedule before the strike, we had nine 3-4 teams to play. These teams have dominating outside linebackers who have taken over the game. When we play the Giants, they have Brad Van Pelt and Lawrence Taylor on the outside. If you try to block Taylor with a back, you're going to lose. It's impossible, so it's better to have two tight ends. Then Lawrence Taylor has to rush around a 250-pound blocker if he wants to get into our backfield. That's a whole different story. With four good receivers, we can also threaten downfield with four men off the line of scrimmage. Miami's defense is doing something that nobody seems to be doing these days, and that's holding down passing teams. They did it against San Diego and they stopped the Jets.

"History gives us a sketch of what a Super Bowl champion is like. I don't think you finesse people to win the Super Bowl. First, it's a team that has a tough, aggressive, physical defense. It paints a picture of a team that's very consistent offensively with a strong running back who doesn't fumble. It's a physical team with a quarterback who's hot, and a team that plays great special teams."

Washington had all those characteristics. Although the Dolphins were the top rated NFL team on defense, the Redskins finished right behind. Theismann, a calmed-down scrambler, finished as the NFC's number one passer; and despite all the times he carried in the playoffs, Riggins never fumbled the ball once. Gibbs was committed to the run. Theismann had a full grasp of the game plan.

"We need the same performance from John Riggins that he has given us all year," Theismann said. "He's our thermometer. If he can run, it opens up other things for us. For example, play-action passes become more convincing, and it's easier to throw. But if they stop the run, they can play pass and concentrate on one element of defense. They begin jamming your receivers. I looked at films of their game against the Jets and didn't see a receiver open all day. We're going to have to do things to get open, but I know we can."

Shula left the assignment of Riggins to his defensive coordinator, Bill Arnsparger, who is so revered by Shula that he gave him the title of assistant coach. Arnsparger has been hailed as a defensive genius, and his accolade was even more

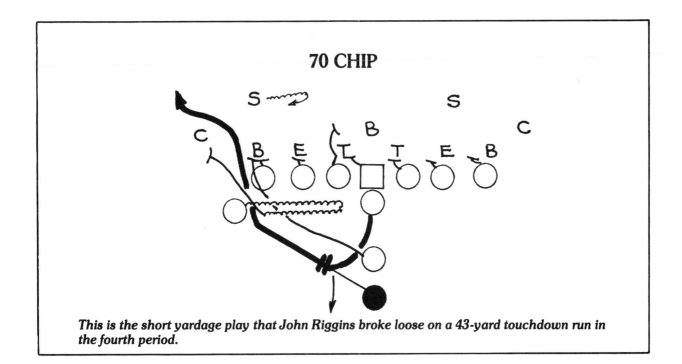

70 CHIP

This is the short yardage play that John Riggins broke loose on a 43-yard touchdown run in the fourth period.

pronounced after the execution of his defensive game plan in completely shutting down the New York Jets, 14-0, in the AFC championship game in the quagmire of the Orange Bowl. That never happened before in a championship. When all was said and done, the Dolphins finished as the number one team against the run in the NFL.

The part of history that Shula and Arnsparger must have discovered disclosed that Washington primarily lived and died by the run. The Redskins won nine straight games in which they ran the ball 49 times or more. In all of their losses, they ran the ball fewer than 30 times. With Washington not expected to play because of a knee injury, it meant that Riggins would be asked to run that much more. Washington had had 80 cc's of fluid drained from his sore knee, which was hobbled by loose cartilage that would require off-season surgery. He was little more than an observer at the Redskins' practice sessions.

"I really haven't worked out much in the last three or four weeks because the knee hasn't had a full year to heal," Washington said. "I can't tell you how badly I want to play in the game. It's just a lot of pain more than anything else."

However, Washington's knee condition wasn't the only problem to be faced. A second storm had been predicted for Friday with clearing anticipated by Saturday afternoon. However, the NFL hierarchy had taken steps to ensure a firm playing field a month before. Immediately after the Rose Bowl game on January 1, the league in-

structed George Toma to begin maintenance on the grass field.

Toma, who has been associated with the Kansas City Chiefs since their membership in the old American Football League, is the acknowledged field maintenance expert around the NFL. With more fields reverting to artificial turf, he is one of the few left who works with grass. He immediately undertook a full reseeding of the Rose Bowl. However, the final work of late seeding, cutting and completing the end zone and midfield designs on the field could only be completed the last week before the Super Bowl. Toma had to get all this done in between raindrops, which caused him to lay two large tarpaulins over the field.

"Give me two days of clear weather and we can have a good, firm field," Toma promised. "Five days and we can have a billiard table."

Toma brought a bit of relief to league headquarters when he telephoned Bill Granholm, supervisor of game logistics for the commissioner's office.

"Mr. Granholm," Toma began, "I just came out from under the tarp. I was crawling around under there for 15 minutes, and I saw a lot of worms. That's a good sign it's growing well. The grass is still tender, but the track will be firm and fast barring an unexpected deluge during the game which nobody can help."

The latest weather report was encouraging despite all the rain.

"If you were playing the game on Saturday or Monday, you'd be in trouble," a weather department official told the NFL.

"I think we're going to be between storms for the game," said NFL Executive Director Don Weiss.

Both coaches minimized any advantage that a wet field would present.

"We have a good offensive line and big power backs who run straight ahead, so weather shouldn't bother us," Shula said. "Besides, Washington has a similar team that can adapt to bad weather."

Gibbs agreed. "I wouldn't think that bad weather would give either team an edge," Gibbs said. "Miami did a good job last week, and we've played in rain a lot this season. The biggest factor could be wind affecting the passing game, wind, and bad footing."

Although Theismann's passing game was slightly diminished when Art Monk, his primary receiver, broke his foot three weeks before the playoffs began, he still had reliable Charlie Brown and an excellent replacement in little Alvin Garrett. During the playoffs, Garrett caught 13 passes for four touchdowns; and Brown contributed 11 with one touchdown. Along with little Virgil Seay, the trio was affectionately named "The Smurfs" after a morning television show.

After his injury, Monk became somewhat of a recluse. Instead of being with his teammates at practice, he stayed away, disappointed that he couldn't contribute more to the team's success. His wife finally convinced him that he would feel better if he could be around the team and offer them some support and encouragement. As a result, Monk once again became a regular at the Redskin practice sessions. With the cast off, he was able to get around a little better at the team's Super Bowl workouts. He felt part of the team again.

"At first, I didn't go to team meetings or come out to practice," Monk admitted. "I didn't watch football on TV or read the papers. I'd jump up in the morning at the time I'd usually go to practice, and then I'd realize that I didn't have to be there. I'd get back in bed, and that's when I'd start thinking about it.

"It really ate me up inside, knowing I couldn't be a part of it. The opportunities are very, very rare. When you're suddenly out of the picture and the rest of your team keeps going, you wish well for them; but it just tears you up inside, knowing that you won't be able to take part in it. I try not to think about it. I try to do other things to keep me laughing.

"When we played the Cowboys last week, I didn't feel as if I was injured. There was so much hype and excitement that I guess I got caught up in it. I actually felt as if I was playing. I'd look at my position, but I'd see Charlie Brown running a pattern. I'd put myself in his shoes, and I'd actually be running off. Then Charlie did something that really touched me, so much that I started to cry. After he caught a touchdown pass, he came over to me on the sidelines and gave the ball to me and we hugged."

Although the Redskins had a more than adequate passing game, they needed the run to make it effective. That meant Riggins. Dry field or not, he would be the main thrust of the offensive surge. Riggins had enjoyed one of his best seasons by running behind a big, mobile line who were popularly called "The Hogs." Halfway through the campaign, Riggins was made a member of The Hogs. In a dressing-room ceremony, Starke gave Riggins a Hogs' shirt, which brought a tear to the big fullback's eyes. Riggins is the only non-lineman who was accorded membership to the group.

"The Hogs are a real bunch of slobs," Riggins said. "They're my kind of guys."

Riggins was John Madden's type of guy. The former Oakland Raider coach has cut out a new career for himself as a color analyst for CBS television. During the playoffs and a couple of times during the season, he had an opportunity to work the Redskin games. Riggins was the type of runner that Madden always believed in. During the telecasts he would always talk about giving the ball to the big guy. Madden felt that Washington would beat Miami, a view not shared by too many others.

"I don't bet; but if I did, my two bucks would be on the Redskins for a couple of reasons," Madden remarked. "It's not that simple; but my gut feeling is that this Super Bowl is going to be a great, old-fashioned football game. Washington's going to win for several reasons, a lot of them having to do with meat-blocking by those Hogs—a victory for bad bodies that does my heart good. I look at them in the locker room, and I want to tell the equipment guy to get me a uniform. But don't be fooled by the lard. Washington's offensive line may be the best in the league.

"Quarterbacks get talked about more than sex, and those receivers do a lot of high flying and get noticed. But what winning a football game like this one is all about is controlling the line of scrim-

Joy is a Super Bowl victory.

mage. Against Miami, Washington is going to do just that. Those bodies might be bad but they're coordinated. They really pick up things well, the stunts and stuff. Riggins figures to run the ball well between the tackles.

"That will make Theismann that much more effective. One of the things Joe Gibbs has done at Washington is make Theismann a quarterback. Before Gibbs got there, Theismann thought he had to win every game himself. He used to run too much and force the pass, which is what gets coaches fired or puts them on television. Theismann finally believes he has ten other guys helping him get it done. He has Riggins and he has a very good offensive line, and he's going to need them against Miami."

Everything pointed to Riggins. Surprisingly, during the regular nine-game season no fewer than 14 other running backs gained more yards in the NFL than Riggins. It only seems fitting that when Riggins is challenged, when he is in the spotlight, he responds like so many other great athletes do. Yet, Mike Hickey, the player personnel director of the New York Jets, tempered the theory.

"If you're talking about John Riggins," Hickey said, "you have to get him interested in football and you have to get him the ball. Those two things. His mind isn't always on the game. He has to be psyched up. He's got to feel wanted. He thrives on being the man. The more often he gets the ball, the better he is. I think he's the most remarkable athlete in the playoffs. At the age of 33, Riggins is the Redskins' workhorse. They've been giving him the ball 30 times a week. How many other 33-year-old workhorses do you know?"

Bill Parcells, defensive coordinator of the New York Giants who was named head coach at season's end, knows all about Riggins. During the season, he had set his defenses twice against Riggins and Washington but failed to defeat the Redskins both times. He had a great deal of respect for Washington and what they accomplished all season.

"Although they are a team that sticks closely to the percentages in their favor, and their offense is a limited one compared to others, the Redskins are going to maneuver in this game," Parcells observed. "But the effectiveness of whatever extra things they try to do will relate to John Riggins, their fullback. If at some point they can get Riggins running, then other opportunities will open up for them. Riggins has great vision. He seldom makes a bad cut, and he can cause tremendous problems. He's a real pain.

"Eighty to ninety percent of the time, the offense will have two tight ends, two wide receivers, and one running back, Riggins. On long yardage plays, it's one tight end, three wide receivers, one running back. However, the Redskins will mix this up and use the three-wide-receiver lineup on first downs when the defense will probably not have a fifth defensive back in the game. Their aim is to match one wide receiver against a strong safety or a linebacker.

"This overall attack may be limited as to the kinds of plays it will try, but it is certainly creative in masking those plays. The defense must know who's in the game at all times, but a defense must not let itself get caught up in figuring out what all the Redskins' looks mean. While this offense was evolving the past two seasons, the Giants played Washington four times. We made a firm decision that we would not let their offensive formations dictate our defense. We were not going to think ourselves out of the game rather than react to the ball."

Yet, that was the ploy that Gibbs planned for Miami. On the plane trip to Los Angeles, he gave Theismann a hint of his strategy against the active Dolphin defense. Gibbs reasoned that if he constantly changed his offensive formations, it would counteract Miami's defensive reads. It didn't invovle a complete overhaul of the offensive strategy that Theismann had executed so successfully up until now. Instead, Gibbs added the wrinkle of shifting the tight end from one side of the formation to the other. At the same time, he would move the wingback, who in most cases was a second tight end anyway, back and forth behind the line of scrimmage while sending the two wide receivers in various motion patterns. Gibbs' intention was to freeze the fluid Miami linebackers to make them react to the distracting movements.

It was a bit of genius on Gibbs' part. He had studied films of Miami's victories over San Diego and the Jets. He had detected how both teams' offenses fell victim to ineptitude by foolishly reacting to the Dolphins' defensive alignments. Both highly offensive teams allowed the Miami defense to dictate to them. It was a costly mistake. Gibbs was clever. The formations, or the plays, he would work from weren't the least bit new. He strongly felt that the motion look would create a problem for the Dolphins.

With each passing day, Gibbs grew more confident that his twist would work. By Thursday morning's quarterback meeting he had added a

For his heroic efforts, Riggins was easily named the game's most valuable player.

new play. Theismann knew something was up when he saw Gibbs smiling.

"Joe had this extra little twinkle in his eye," Theismann said. "You just knew that he had something special, like a kid with a new toy. The coaches called it 'The Explode Package.' It was a series of four plays in which we've got everybody in the world moving. The tight end moves from split to tight; the wingback moves from the right side to the left side; the halfback moves from behind me to behind the tight end; the two wide receivers shift out, and one of them goes in motion. All of this happens when I say 'set.' It looks like a Chinese fire drill.

"It fit right in with our game plan. It was just another way to confuse the Dolphins. Defense works by recognition; and when you inhibit that recognition by getting everyone moving around, you get the defense saying, 'Now wait a second. Where is everybody?' This particular package was designed for what we call the Red Area—inside Miami's 20-yard line. But even if we never got close to the goal line all day, Joe said he wanted to use it anyway, just to hear what the TV announcers would say when they saw everybody moving."

It was doubtful that if anybody else learned of Gibbs' ploy that it would have bought any more respect for the Redskins. Earlier in the week, the nation's oddsmakers had established them as three-point underdogs, a margin that remained right until game time. Apparently most of the bettors agreed with the professional oddsmakers and wagered their money on the Dolphins who, along with Don Shula's achievements, had caught the public's fancy. In addition the New York *Daily News* conducted a poll among the league's coaches. Of the 18 coaches participating, 13 picked Miami to win. The Redskins couldn't even generate support within its own conference where six of the nine coaches polled felt that the Dolphins would win Super Bowl XVII. Even Parcells and Landry agreed.

"Washington's strength revolves around John Riggins," Parcells said. "Miami's strength revolves around its defensive front. Miami has an

Burt Wallach, a bartender in the Georgetown sector of Washington, serves patrons during the Super Bowl game in a Redskin headdress.

Owner Jack Kent Cooke, second from left, holds the game ball and Super Bowl trophy in Redskins' dressing room. With Cooke are, from left, Joe Theismann, John Riggins and Joe Gibbs.

overall edge defensively and is a little more talented."

Landry also felt the Dolphins' defense was better. "Miami's defense has been too consistent and performed too well not to go with them," Landry said.

The five coaches who felt that Washington would win were Ed Biles of Houston, Walt Michaels of the New York Jets, Bum Phillips of New Orleans, Marion Campbell of Philadelphia and Jim Hanifan of St. Louis.

Yet, of the minority who liked Washington's chances, two were unique. One was Danny Sheridan, a sports analyst for *USA Today*, who does his research in his office in Mobile, Alabama. He picked Washington even without the points in his column. Appearing on a local television show in Los Angeles, he added a final twist to his selection.

"Why are you picking Washington?" asked the show's host.

"Because my fiancée likes them," Sheridan answered.

"You have to be kidding?" came the reply.

"No, sir. It's the truth. My fiancée wrote Don Shula a letter over a month ago, and he never answered her. She told me to make sure I pick Washington to win the Super Bowl, and I did."

Oddly, Dewey Wong, Sheridan's friend from New York, picked Washington for a far different reason. Wong, who owns a restaurant bearing his name, told a group of reporters that the Redskins would win.

"In Chinese New York next week," Wong began, "it is the Year of the Pig. They call the Washington linemen the Hogs, so it all ties together. I've never seen it to fail when such a similarity appeared in past Super Bowls."

The run that shook the world. On a crucial fourth and one situation in the fourth period, Riggins breaks away from Miami cornerback Don McNeal on his way to the game-winning 43-yard touchdown run.

One element that didn't fail, fortunately, was the weather. Super Sunday dawned with the promise of a dry day. By mid-morning the sun was shining brightly, taking some pressure off Toma. At six o'clock that morning he had pulled the tarpaulins off the field and allowed the sun to evaporate any moisture that the week-long rains had left. There was no indication that the field would present any particular problem to either team. All morning long radio and television announcers urged those fans who were going to the game to make sure they arrived at the Rose Bowl site early to allow for bad traffic conditions in certain areas. They advised that public transportation would be best since parking was definitely a problem due to the heavy rains that had flooded open areas near the stadium.

Apparently the fans listened. Five hours before the 3 p.m. kickoff, most of the expected crowd of 103,000 had made themselves comfortable. Those who had arrived by automobiles were involved with the familiar tailgate parties while those already in the big bowl did their eating and drinking in their seats. The roar of the crowd after both teams appeared for their pre-

game warm-ups indicated that the fans were partial to the Redskins.

As the home team, Washington chose to wear their white jerseys with their maroon pants. This left the Dolphins to dress in their green jerseys and white trousers. The coin-toss ceremony at midfield resembled a convention. There were three Dolphins on one side, while the Redskins sent no fewer than eight representatives to the confab, including Peter Cronan, Monte Coleman, Joe Lavender, Joe Theismann, Dave Butz, Mark Murphy, George Starke and Joe Washington. The Dolphins' Bob Kuechenberg told referee Jerry Markbreit that he would call the toss and preferred heads. The coin came up heads, but Markbreit signaled that Washington had won the toss. Kuechenberg quickly corrected him and said that the Dolphins would receive the kickoff. The referee then made a second mistake. He lined up the players and signaled that the Redskins would receive. Again Kuechenberg corrected him. Miami would handle the opening kickoff to start Super Bowl XVII.

The roar of the crowd, standing on its feet, accompanied Mark Moseley's stride as he booted

Near the end of the dramatic run, Riggins is all alone as he nears the end zone.

Joe Theismann avoided what would have been a disastrous third period touchdown by Miami. After Dolphin defensive end Kim Bokamper deflected Theismann's pass, he started to catch the ball in mid-air on about the five-yard line. Theismann alertly ran over and knocked the ball out of Bokamper's hands.

the ball at 3:17 p.m. and began Washington's journey into the history books. Lyle Blackwood caught the ball on the eight-yard line and brought it back to the 25. The jitters that always occur prior to the first physical contact of a game were now relieved. Young quarterback Dave Woodley, who had played outstandingly in the playoffs, gathered the Dolphins in their first offensive huddle.

The Dolphins planned to open the game with a pass, nothing deep, but a short one to running

back Tony Nathan. It failed. Andra Franklin tried the Washington middle and picked up two yards. It was time to pass again. Woodley intended to do so but finding no one open, scrambled for seven yards to the 34, just a yard short of a first down. Miami had to punt.

Mike Nelms, who doesn't know what a fair catch is, did what he always does, and ran with a punt. He took Tom Orosz's kick on the 24 and returned it to the 29. Theismann's first call was practically automatic. He handed the ball to Riggins, and the big fullback surged straight ahead for five yards. Riggins got the ball again and went through right tackle for four yards. On third down it was Riggins again. This time he turned right end for three yards and a first down on the 41-yard line. Then Theismann switched. He hit Brown with a quick swing pass that gathered 11 yards to the Miami 48-yard line. After Riggins could only gain a yard, Theismann's medium range pass to Garrett at the Miami 28-yard line was incomplete. When he tried to pass on third down, Theismann was sacked for a seven-yard loss on the Redskin 46 by linebacker Earnie Rhone. It meant that Jeff Hayes would punt, and he boomed his kick into the Dolphin end zone.

On first down Woodley used Nathan again, only this time on a running play which gained four yards to the 24. Turning to the pass, Woodley sent wide receiver Jimmy Cefalo in motion to the right. He dropped back, looked away from Cefalo, and a few seconds later looked back to him. Woodley couldn't believe his eyes. Cefalo got past cornerback Jeris White, who had the short coverage in the zone. However, safety Tony Peters, who was supposed to drop back off the tight end and pick up Cefalo, didn't. Cefalo was all alone when he caught Woodley's pass on the Miami 45 and could hardly contain his joy as he ran the rest of the way for a touchdown. The sudden strike stunned the big crowd as well as the Redskins. Uwe Von Schamann, who had been bothered by a bad back for two weeks, added the extra point that gave the Dolphins a 7-0 lead.

Washington went back to work following the kickoff in the same methodical manner in which they challenged their opponents all season long. Starting from the 25, Riggins got four yards up the middle and then went back the same way and got five more. Just when it appeared that Washington was about to produce a first down, Theismann was sacked by linebacker Larry Gordon on the 31. Hayes punted again, and Miami got the ball on its own 38-yard line with six minutes left in the opening period.

Nathan quickly got the Dolphins to midfield with a 12-yard burst through the center of the Redskin defense. Franklin went the same direction and shook loose for nine yards. When the big fullback added four more off left tackle, the Dolphins had a first down on the Washington 27 and appeared ready to strike again. The Redskins would be at a distinct disadvantage if Miami moved for another touchdown and swept to a 14-0 lead. That was foremost in Dexter Manley's mind. Throughout the season he had produced

the big play on defense. He stared at Woodley barking the signals. At the snap count, he pushed tackle Jon Giesler aside and charged straight toward Woodley, who dropped back to pass. Woodley didn't have a chance. Manley buried him, and the ball popped loose as Woodley was crashing to earth. It rolled behind Woodley all the way back to the Miami 46-yard line where Butz recovered the ball for Washington. It was a big turnover, and the Redskin defense came off the field to the cheers of the crowd.

Theismann quickly went to the air. However, he just missed on a timing pattern with Brown, who caught the ball as he stepped out of bounds. Switching back to the run on second and long, Theismann had Miami thinking pass again and sent Clarence Harmon through the left side for eight yards. When Theismann fired a short three-yard pass to Don Warren, the Redskins had a first down on the Dolphins' 35.

Riggins then went to work. In four straight assaults over left tackle, Riggins got six, seven, four, and three yards. When the action finally subsided in the first period, Washington had reached the Miami 15-yard line.

Beginning the second-quarter play, Theismann faced a third and three situation. The strategy was to run Riggins again. However, on his fifth consecutive carry he could only gain a yard; and the Redskins had to settle for a field goal. Mark Moseley gave it to them when he booted a 31-yarder off Theismann's hold to trim Miami's edge to 7-3.

Return specialist Fulton Walker gave the Dolphins excellent field position when he took Hayes' kickoff on the five-yard line and ran it back 42 yards to the 47, nearly breaking it for a touchdown. Nathan took a pitchout for eight yards and then picked up three more up the middle for a first down on the Washington 42. After Franklin was held to a yard, Woodley hit Duriel Harris with an eight-yard pass to the 33. Franklin then picked up the first down when he bulled his way to the 31. Miami was mounting another scoring threat. A Woodley to Cefalo pass got six yards; Nathan lost a yard. But on third down, throwing out of the shotgun, Woodley connected with Harris for a big first down on the 19-yard line.

Franklin made four yards to the 15. A Washington offsides penalty put the Redskins further in the hole at the 10. When Franklin gained two yards, Miami had a first down on the eight-yard line. The pressure was on the Redskin defense to hold. Franklin got two tough yards. Woodley tried to roll around right end but was stopped by Mark Murphy on the three. On third down, Woodley looked for Cefalo; but Vernon Dean was ready for the challenge and knocked the pass away. Von Schamann entered the game and booted a 20-yard field goal that stretched Miami's margin to 10-3.

There was 5:55 remaining in the first half when Washington put the kickoff in play on the 20-yard line after Von Schamann boomed the ball out of the end zone. Theismann got the Redskins moving with a 27-yard pass to Walker. He used Walker on a reverse, and the big tight end playing before his hometown fans gained six yards. Riggins then got three yards and picked up a first down on his next carry when he gained a yard to the Miami 43.

Throwing on first down, Theismann hooked up with Brown on a swing pass that gained four yards. On second down, Theismann made use of his scrambling ability. He scrambled to his left, stopped, and threw back to his right to Riggins who got to the 24-yard line. The Redskins were in excellent position to secure the tying touchdown with just over three minutes left. They experienced a temporary setback when Riggins lost a yard. Theismann rectified the situation when, after attempting to pass, he scrambled for 12 yards and a first down on the 13. Riggins kept the Redskin fans cheering when he broke inside for six yards to the seven as the clock reached the two-minute mark and an automatic time out. Theismann conferred with Gibbs on the sidelines and returned to the huddle. Riggins was sent around left end and moved for three yards. Then it happened. Theismann called the Explode Package, the formation that Gibbs had inserted into the game plan on Thursday. There was all kinds of movement going on as Theismann took a short drop to pass. He threw to Garrett in the end zone for the tying touchdown as the Dolphin defenders looked around in bewilderment. Moseley added the conversion that deadlocked the contest at 10-10.

The fervor of the fans continued as Walker added to their enthusiasm. He settled under Hayes' kickoff on the two-yard line, making a move to his left on the seven-yard line and turning on a burst of speed that got him past a converging group of Redskins. When he reached the 40-yard line, it was apparent that nobody could catch him. Walker never stopped until he reached the end zone with a 98-yard kickoff return for a record Super Bowl touchdown. It created disbelief among the Redskin special team members.

They had let the Dolphins off the hook, and what should have been a tied game at halftime, turned into a Miami advantage following Von Schamann's extra point that sent the AFC champions into a 17-10 lead.

There was just 1:34 on the clock when Washington got the ball back on offense. An illegal block on the kickoff put them in the hole on the seven-yard line. The Redskins had to avoid any mistake at this point. Riggins got three yards and Harmon added four. Theismann scrambled for 19 yards and a first down on the 24. A short pass to Don Warren realized four yards. A Dolphin mistake brought the Redskins into an attacking position. Safety Lyle Blackwood was too aggressive on pass defense and interfered with Nick Giaquinto's attempt to catch Theismann's aerial. He was flagged for the infraction which gave Washington a first down on the Miami 42. There were just 30 seconds left, and the Redskins didn't have any timeouts remaining. They had to act without delay. Theismann connected with Brown on the Dolphin 16-yard line. Only 14 seconds left. The Redskins didn't huddle; there wasn't any time. Theismann fired to Garrett on the eight-yard line. He was too far inside from the sidelines to get out of bounds and stop the clock. Theismann was helpless to try to get off one more play. After coming so close, the Redskins were swept with frustration as the referee signaled a halt to the first half's action in which they trailed 17-10.

Washington's frustration was further underlined in the statistics. They had 12 first downs to Miami's seven, had gained 191 yards to 142, and ran off 35 plays to 22. If it hadn't been for two big plays, one of 76 yards and another of 98, the Dolphins very possibly might not have scored two touchdowns.

Still, there was no reason to panic or to deviate from the game plan. Gibbs didn't say much to his players at halftime. He really didn't have to. The team was playing well and being behind seven points at this moment wasn't catastrophic. Gibbs was in total control. He calmly moved some pass plays from second down priority up to first to overcome Miami's run defense. Then he spoke to the entire squad just before they went back on the field.

"We've been down by more than seven points before," he reminded them. "We were down 11 points to the Giants and beat them. Champions can come back and win."

The second half didn't start promisingly for the Redskins despite their taking the kickoff back to their 33-yard line. Riggins lost a yard, and Theis-

Redskin fans celebrate Super Bowl triumph by climbing aboard a Washington Metro bus.

mann was sacked for a nine-yard loss on the very next play. When Theismann failed on a third down pass attempt to Brown, Hayes had to punt. His kick wasn't very good, but the Redskins were aided by a 15-yard penalty that placed the ball on the Miami 31. Franklin opened with a nine-yard run. After Nathan was stopped for no gain, Woodley used a quarterback sneak to pick up a yard and a first down on the 41. A pass failed. Franklin then gained four yards, but Woodley again missed on a pass play. Orosz's punt wasn't

very long, and Nelms' 12-yard return gave the Redskins the ball on the 36-yard line.

Theismann worked a swing pass with Warren that netted seven yards. Riggins broke loose for four yards and a first down on the 47. The Redskins needed a spark. They got it on the very next play. On a well-disguised reverse, Theismann handed the ball to Riggins and the Miami defense reacted. However, Riggins gave the ball to Garrett, and the speedy receiver had an open field in front of him around left end. He raced all the way down to the Miami nine-yard line before he was tackled from behind by cornerback Gerald Small.

Washington was primed for the tying touchdown. The Dolphins were waiting for Riggins and stopped him after a two-yard advance. It was time to pass. Warren caught a short four-yard toss on the three-yard line. Theismann had to go into the end zone with the next one, and he overthrew Garrett. Moseley was sent in for a field goal, and he responded with a 20-yard kick that narrowed Miami's advantage to 17-13.

The Dolphins couldn't do anything after the kickoff when Nathan was stopped without a gain, and Woodley missed on two passes and had to punt. Even though Washington took possession on its own 48, they couldn't do anything. Riggins got four yards on two carries, and Theismann was inaccurate on a third down pass. The Dolphins were ineffective also. Two rushes by Franklin yielded six yards. Trying to pass for the first down, Woodley was off target; and Orosz had to punt once more.

There was 3:55 left in the third period when Theismann and the offense returned to the field on the Washington 38-yard line. In just one play they were back off. Trying to loft a pass to Warren on the 47, Theismann underthrew the tight end; and linebacker A. J. Duhe intercepted. Miami had an excellent opportunity to add to its lead. An offsides infraction by Washington moved the ball to the 42. Woodley then scrambled for a first down to the 37. The Redskins had to stop Miami's threat. Butz contributed when he dropped Franklin for a two-yard loss. On second down, a pass was anticipated as Washington inserted a fifth defensive back. Woodley took a deep drop. He had time as he looked downfield. He threw to Cefalo on the five-yard line; but Dean deflected the ball, and the alert Murphy caught it before it hit the ground for a big interception with 2:42 left.

Theismann turned to Riggins to get the Redskins out of danger. He did so by running for nine yards and then four more and a first down on the 18. Then Theismann almost made the biggest mistake of the game. Attempting to pass, he scrambled around and back to the seven-yard line. Finally, he got off a weak pass to his left. Defensive end Kim Bokamper tipped the ball into the air and started to grab it. He seemed to be headed for a touchdown. However, the determined Theismann ran over in time to knock the ball out of Bokamper's hands, averting a disastrous touchdown. The Washington quarterback breathed a sigh of relief before the next play in

Charlie Brown signals the end for Miami. He scored Washington's final touchdown in the closing minutes of the game.

which Harmon broke loose for 12 yards to the 30. All the Redskins felt better. The third period ended two plays later after Riggins gained two yards and Theismann's short pass to Brown added four more.

Theismann began the fourth quarter with a ten-yard completion to Warren and a first down on the 46-yard line. The Redskins were moving. Riggins made sure by breaking loose behind center Jeff Bostic for nine yards. Then he got two more and another first down on the Miami 43. Suddenly, without warning, a Redskins' trick play backfired. Theismann handed to Riggins who ran straight ahead, stopped before he reached the line of scrimmage, and lateraled the ball to Theismann. The play didn't fool the Dolphins. When Theismann tried to throw deep downfield to Brown, safety Lyle Blackwood was waiting and intercepted the ball on the one-yard line. Redskin hearts sank.

It was up to the Washington defense to keep the Dolphins pinned down, and they did. After Franklin could only gain three yards on two carries and Woodley still couldn't complete a pass in the second half, Miami had to punt. Orosz had a pressure punt from his end zone but, nevertheless, got the ball out to the 45-yard line. An illegal block by the Redskins placed the ball further back to the Redskin 48.

Time wasn't a factor yet as 11:43 remained.

Running left, Riggins got the Washington offense going with a seven-yard advance to the Miami 45. He added another yard to the 44. On third down, Theismann switched to Harmon; but he was stopped after a yard pickup. On fourth and one, Washington decided to go for it from the Miami 43. Surprisingly at that juncture, the Dolphins called time out. When play was resumed, Miami lined up in its goal line defense. They had ten players on the line of scrimmage with only cornerback Don McNeil backing up the line. Everybody in the Rose Bowl and the countless millions watching on television knew that Riggins, who had now gained more than 100 yards in the game, would carry the ball.

The most dramatic moment of the game had the crowd squirming in excitement. Theismann began his rhythmic chant. Clint Didier, an extra tight end, went in motion toward the middle and then started back to his left. McNeal followed him and slipped. The alert Theismann hurried the count to take advantage of McNeal's misfortune. Theismann quickly handed the ball to Riggins. Little Otis Wonsley, the chunky 214-pound back, made contact with the first Dolphin he reached. Riggins slid along the left side of the line and then broke toward the outside. A lunging McNeal tried to grab him with an arm, but it was useless. Riggins headed down the sideline with no one in front of him. Glenn Blackwood tried to give chase, but Riggins kept pulling away from him and turned a short yardage play into an electrifying 43-yard touchdown. The crowd was in a frenzy. Even after Moseley added the conversion that sent the Redskins in front for the first time, 20-17, the crowd was still buzzing about Riggins' run to daylight. Washington's defense was really fired up now. Miami's next series of downs was vital, and the relentless Redskins repelled their efforts. From the 22, Franklin managed three yards; but Harris could only get one on a reverse. When Woodley's third down pass was knocked down by Joe Lavender, Redskin fans cheered. Miami had no choice but to punt.

Nelms' 12-yard punt return provided the Redskins with prime field position on the Miami 41. Washington wanted more points, at least a field goal. Riggins started the drive like a man possessed, as if he knew that he was destined to have his place in pro-football history. Five straight times he lugged the ball, gaining six, three, two, and seven yards before he was finally stopped for no gain on the 23. He was wearing down the Dolphin defense with each carry. Harmon got four yards and a Washington first down on the 19.

Then it was Riggins again for a yard. After Harmon was stopped, Theismann kept the drive going with a nine-yard pass to Brown on the nine. Once again Theismann turned to Riggins. He got three yards to the six. When he carried again, he was stopped without any further advance. The automatic two-minute warning was signaled, and Theismann utilized the timeout to talk with Gibbs near the Redskin bench. Washington could feel the victory. It was ever so close. Theismann joined the huddle and shouted "explode." The Redskins broke, and five different players went in motion as Theismann called the signals. He took the snap, rolled to his right, and threw a pass to Brown in the end zone just before he fell out of bounds. The delirious Redskins mobbed Brown for the high-five touchdown ceremony. Moseley calmly added the conversion to send Washington into an insurmountable 27-17 lead.

It made no difference that Don Strock replaced Woodley, who hadn't completed a single pass in the second half. It was too late. It was of little consequence that as the clock clicked down to 1:12, Tommy Vigorito got four yards, because Strock missed all three passes he threw from the Miami 39-yard line. This was the greatest moment in Redskin history. Harmon closed it out with three carries of three, four, and five yards. Theismann handled the ball for the last time when he broke the snap and fell to the ground. By now everybody in America knew that the pigskin belonged to the Hogs. At 6:29 Pacific Coast Time, the Hogs and the Smurfs and the wonderful bunch of Redskins were champions of the world.

In the small, steamy cubicle that was their dressing room, the Redskins knelt in prayer. It was in keeping with their character all season long. Gibbs wouldn't have it any other way. Later, 3,000 miles from home, the shouting and the celebration that would last long into the California night could begin. It was a time for unrestrained joy, a feeling none of these Redskins had ever experienced before. Hail to the Redskins, indeed! The respect that had been denied them all year was now theirs.

Riggins was escorted out of the dressing room to an adjacent press room across the way to a makeshift interview area where reporters were tightly bunched together. Riggins had been unanimously voted the game's most valuable player. He seemed unaffected by it all as he made it to his seat on a hastily assembled platform.

"Ron may be the President, but I'm the king," Riggins quipped. "I'm very happy, at least for tonight."

In the next 20 minutes or so, Riggins didn't elaborate on any of the questions asked of him except one. A writer wanted to know if he was worried going into the game knowing so much was expected of him. Riggins smiled, leaving the impression that he had the answer waiting all along.

"I was camping out one night," he replied, "with an old fella named Glenn Jenkins back in Centralia, Kansas. I could hear the coyotes howling, and they sounded like they were getting mighty close. I asked Glenn if he felt nervous. He said, 'I've probably killed 200 of them. It doesn't exactly raise the hair on the back of my neck.' It's like the NFL games. I've probably gone through 130 of them, and they don't exactly raise the hair on the back of my neck."

It created laughter among some of the press. Then Riggins turned to his performance and the game itself.

"How many carries did I have?" he wanted to know.

"Thirty-eight," came the reply.

"That's on the verge of too many," Riggins said. "I'm very happy, but I'm very tired. I told Joe Gibbs I wanted the ball against Detroit, but I think he got a little carried away."

"Describe the touchdown play," asked someone.

"It's a play we ran all season," Riggins explained. "It's called 70-Chip out of the I formation. If you went back, you'd see that we ran it seven or eight times against Dallas last week. If we can get through the line, we can make a big play. I told Joe Theismann that we were close to breaking it several times."

"What about your speed on the 43-yard touchdown run?" came another question.

"I broke a tackle and got outside," Riggins answered. "I could go on about my speed, but no one would believe me."

"How were the Hogs today?" asked another.

"Magnificent," Riggins exclaimed. "I might take them out to dinner or something when we get back to D.C., but it's a little early to tell what I'll do for them. The real crime is that none of our interior linemen were picked for the Pro-Bowl."

Before Riggins left to get dressed, he surprised his audience by telling them that the team's owner had decided to present the players with bracelets instead of the customary diamond rings that have been emblematic of Super Bowl champions.

"Jack Kent Cooke is the only guy with enough

Joe Theismann tells the world who is No. 1.

186

imagination to give us bracelets instead of rings," Riggins said. "They'll probably have 30 or 40 diamonds of one carat each."

Gibbs was brought into the room and talked to the media. No one appreciated Riggins more than the Washington coach.

"I told my players that this game will be won by John," Gibbs said. "But all the things that go with it, the flea flicker, the reverse, all those will help John. We've got to keep them off him. John Riggins is the only guy I know who can carry you to the Super Bowl by carrying the ball 30 to 35 times a game. Some other guys carry 20 times, and they can't walk the next day. John has lost only one fumble in the two years he has been with me.

"Actually, I was thinking about the play he ran for a touchdown on third down. We knew if we didn't make it on third down, it would be a risky field goal. We felt we would take our best play and go at them. We felt we didn't want to lose a Super Bowl game by not being tough enough. John made a great run. We didn't want to play to avoid losing. We wanted to be aggressive and do all the things we do well so we could run Riggins.

"I think some people have underestimated us because we're a total team. We've been kind of a tough physical team, and I think that's what you've got to do to win the Super Bowl. I was a little surprised we were able to move the ball as well as we did. This is a total team effort, all of our fans and everybody pulling together. Part of this goes back to every Redskin fan back home who helped us get here. I want to thank first of all God, second Mr. Cooke, Bobby Beathard, our fans back home, and our players. I'm just thankful for all those people in that order. God first."

The joy on Theismann's face was there for anyone to see. He exuded boyish happiness and, at the same time, relief when recalling two key plays in which he was directly involved. He talked about the pass just before the half and later about the one that was almost intercepted for a touchdown in the fourth period.

"Right before the half I knew I made a stupid play," Theismann said. "I thought with 14 seconds left we could get the play off in time to try a field goal, but the biggest play of the game to me was when I knocked the interception out of Bokamper's hands. I saw the ball up in the air, and I could just see him going for it and running for a touchdown. I just sort of dove and tried to get in the middle between him and the ball.

"The key to this game was our ability to run the ball. If Riggins runs well, it opens up the passing game for us. We just turned our Hogs loose today. I am very confident about this football team. It's not one or two men; it's everybody contributing. The guys up front did a great job for John. The special teams came through when they had to, and the defense shut them [Miami] down all afternoon.

"I'm a very emotional player, and this whole thing is a dream come true for me. I mean, I can't believe it. This is everything I've always wanted as a person and as a player—everything. There's a ton of little kid in this 33-year-old body. You can say, 'Look at that idiot out there rolling around on the grass with Charlie Brown,' and you know what? I don't care."

What the Hogs had cared about at halftime was getting Riggins to run with the ball the way they felt he could. Center Jeff Bostic made that much clearer.

"When we came out in the third quarter, we wanted to make John very tough running the ball and make the corners and safeties tackle him," Bostic said. "I think it was evident in the third quarter just how tough John was running the ball. His touchdown run, I think, broke their back. It wasn't so much what it did for our club—it was what it did against their team. I could feel their tempo drop as a result of the touchdown run."

Guard Russ Grimm, who plays alongside Bostic, felt the same way. He shared the same confidence as the rest of the offensive line in giving Riggins the chance to run.

"We knew we could do it," Grimm said. "It was just a matter of time. We just started out pounding away in the second half. John has been running well throughout the playoffs after being kind of up and down during the regular season. I don't want to be the guy who lets him down. Big John doesn't say a whole lot. He says 'thank you' to us, and that means a lot. He's really a low-key person. It's a privilege to block for him."

Dave Butz, the big defensive tackle, perhaps put it all into perspective about the entire Washington team. They think and play as a team.

"You knew someone would come up with the big play today," Butz said. "We play as a team and don't rely on superstars. Being number one, you can't be any higher. If we were any higher we'd be in heaven."

Bobby Beathard knew the feeling. He walked out of the cavernous Rose Bowl through a tunnel filled with Redskin fans with his arm around his father into the dark California night. He was so happy that he didn't even notice the crowd. This night belonged to the Redskins.　●

JANUARY 30, 1983
ROSE BOWL
PASADENA, CALIFORNIA

SCORE BY PERIODS

Miami . . . . 7 10 0 0—17
Washington . . . . 0 10 3 14—27

SCORING

Miami—Cefalo 76 pass from Woodley
   (von Schamann kick).
Washington—Field goal Moseley 31.
Miami—Field goal von Schamann 20.
Washington—Garrett 4 pass from Theismann
   (Moseley kick).
Miami—Walker 98 kickoff return
   (von Schamann kick).
Washington—Field goal Moseley 20.
Washington—Riggins 43 run (Moseley kick).
Washington—Brown 6 pass from Theismann
   (Moseley kick).

TEAM STATISTICS

	Miami	Wash.
FIRST DOWNS	9	24
By Rushing.	7	14
By Passing	2	9
By Penalty	0	1
THIRD-DOWN EFFICIENCY	3-11	11-18
FOURTH-DOWN EFFICIENCY	0-1	1-1
TOTAL NET YARDS	176	400
Total Off. Plays	47	78
Avg. Gain Per Play	3.7	5.1
NET YARDS RUSHING. . .	96	276
Total Rushing PLays. . . .	29	52
Avg. Gain Per Rush	3.3	5.3
NET YARDS PASSING . . .	80	124
Sacks—Yards Lost	1-17	3-19
Gross Yards Passing	97	143
PASSES	4-17-1	15-23-2
Avg. Gain Per Pass.	4.4	4.8
PUNTS	6-37.8	4-42.0
Had Blocked	0	0
TOTAL RET. YARDS	244	109
Punt Returns	2-22	6-52
Kickoff Returns	6-222	3-57
Interception Ret.	2-0	1-0
PENALTIES—YARDS	4-55	5-36
FUNBLES—LOST	2-1	0-0
TIME OF POSS.	23:45	36:15

Attendance—103,667.

INDIVIDUAL STATISTICS

Rushing—Miami, Franklin 16-49, Nathan 7-26,
   Woodley 4-16, Vigorito 1-4, Harris 1-1;
   Washington, Riggins 30-166, Garrett 1-44,
   Harmon 9-40, Theismann 3-20, Walker 1-6.
Passing—Miami, Woodley 4-14-1—97, Strock 0-
   3-0—0; Washington, Theismann 15-23-2—
   143.
Receiving—Miami, Cefalo 2-82, Harris 2-15;
   Washington, Brown 6-60, Warren 5-28,
   Garrett 2-13, Walker 1-27, Riggins 1-15.
Kickoff Returns—Miami, Walker 4-190, L.
   Blackwood 2-32; Washington, Nelms 2-44,
   Wonsley 1-13.
Punt Returns—Miami, Vigorito 2-22;
   Washington, Nelms 6-52.
Interception Returns—Miami, Duhe 1-0, L.
   Blackwood 1-0; Washington, Murphy 1-0.
Punting—Miami, Orosz 6-37.8; Washington,
   Hayes 4-42.0.

REGULAR SEASON
WASHINGTON REDSKINS STATISTICS

RESULTS AND ATTENDANCE (Actual)

(WON 8, LOST 1)

(W) 37	at Philadelphia Eagles (OT)	34	68,885
(W) 21	at Tampa Bay	13	66,187
(W) 27	at New York Giants	17	70,766
(W) 13	Philadelphia Eagles	9	48,313
(L) 10	Dallas Cowboys	24	54,633
(W) 12	St. Louis Cardinals	7	35,308
(W) 15	New York Giants	14	50,030
(W) 27	at New Orleans Saints	10	48,667
(W) 28	St. Louis Cardinals	0	52,554

TEAM STATISTICS

TEAM STATISTICS	Redskins	Opponent
TOTAL FIRST DOWNS	165	150
Rushing	66	46
Passing	87	93
Penalty	12	11
3rd Down: Made/Att.	55-133	40-115
4th Down: Made/Att.	2-3	1-5
TOTAL NET YARDS	2985	2560
Avg. Per Game	331.7	284.4
Total Plays	598	554
Avg. Per Play	5.0	4.6
NET YARDS RUSHING	1140	946
Avg. Per Game	126.7	105.1
Total Rushes	315	247
NET YARDS PASSING	1845	1614
Avg. Per Game	205.0	179.3
Tackled/Yards Lost	30-223	32-256
Gross Yards	2068	1870
Attempts/Completions	253-162	275-146
Pct. of Completions	64.0	53.1
Had Intercepted	9	11
PUNTS/AVERAGE	52-37.3	57-39.4
NET PUNTING AVG.	33.3	33.2
PENALTIES/YARDS	46-404	52-572
FUMBLES/BALL LOST	15-7	23-13
TOUCHDOWNS	19	16
Rushing	5	8
Passing	13	8
Returns	1	0

SCORE BY PERIODS

	1	2	3	4	OT	Total
REDSKINS TOTAL	36	67	22	62	3	190
Opp. Total	17	33	43	35	0	128

SCORING

SCORING	TDR	TDP	TDRt	PAT	FG	S	TP
Mark Moseley				16-19	20-21		76
Charlie Brown		8					48
John Riggins	3						18
Joe Washington	1	1					12
Art Monk		1					6
Curtis Jordan			1				6
Otis Wonsley		1					6
Clarence Harmon	1						6
Clint Didier		1					6
Rick Walker		1					6
REDSKIN TOTAL	5	13	1	16-19	20-21		190
Opp. Total	8	8	0	14-16	6-9		128

FIELD GOALS

FIELD GOALS	1-19	20-29	30-39	40-49	50+	Total
Mark Moseley	1-1	6-6	8-8	5-6	0-0	20-21
REDSKINS TOTAL	1-1	6-6	8-8	5-6	0-0	20-21
Opp. Total	0-0	1-2	2-2	3-4	0-1	6-9

PASSING

PASSING	Att.	Comp.	Yards	Pct.	Avg./Att.	TD	Pct. TD	Int.	Pct. Int.	LG	Lost/Att.	Rating
Joe Theismann	252	161	2033	63.9	8.07	13	5.2	9	3.6	78t	30-223	91.3
Joe Washington	1	1	35	100.0	35.00	0	0.0	0	0.0	35	0-0	—
REDSKINS TOTAL	253	162	2068	64.0	8.17	13	5.1	9	3.6	78t	30-223	91.5
Opp. Total	275	146	1970	53.1	7.2	8	2.9	11	4.0	62t	32-256	69.3

RUSHING

RUSHING	No.	Yds.	Avg.	LG	TD
John Riggins	177	553	3.1	19	3
Joe Washington	44	190	4.3	40	1
Clarence Harmon	38	168	4.4	20	1
Joe Theismann	31	150	4.8	16	0
Otis Wonsley	11	36	3.3	7	0
Art Monk	7	21	3.0	14	0
Rick Walker	2	11	5.5	6	0
Wilbur Jackson	4	6	1.5	2	0
Nick Giaquinto	1	5	5.0	5	0
REDSKINS TOTAL	315	1140	3.6	40	5
Opp. Total	247	946	3.8	64	8

RECEIVING

RECEIVING	No.	Yds.	Avg.	LG	TD
Art Monk	35	447	12.8	43	1
Charlie Brown	32	690	21.6	78t	8
Don Warren	27	310	11.5	29	0
Joe Washington	19	134	7.1	17	1
Rick Walker	12	92	7.7	25	1
Clarence Harmon	11	86	7.8	28	0
John Riggins	10	50	5.0	11	0
Virgil Seay	6	154	25.7	37	0
Mike Williams	3	14	3.7	6	0
Nick Giaquinto	2	65	32.5	29	0
Didier/Wonsley	2/1	10/1	5.0/1.0	8/1	1/1
Jackson/Garrett	1/1	9/6	9.0/6.0	9/6	0/0
REDSKINS TOTAL	162	2068	12.8	78t	13
Opp. Total	146	1870	13.5	62	8

INTERCEPTIONS

INTERCEPTIONS	No.	Yds.	Avg.	LG	TD
Vernon Dean	3	62	20.7	26	0
Jeris White	3	4	1.3	4	0
Mark Murphy	2	0	0.0	0	0
Tony Peters	1	14	14.0	14	0
L. McDaniel	1	7	7.0	7	0
Dexter Manley	1	−2	−2.0	−2	0
REDSKINS TOTAL	11	85	7.7	26	0
Opp. Total	9	68	7.6	15	0

PUNTING

PUNTING	No.	Yds.	Avg.	TB	In 20	LG	Blk.
Jeff Hayes	51	1937	38.0	5	10	58	1
REDSKINS TOTAL	51	1937	38.0	5	10	58	1
Opp. Total	56	2247	40.1	3	5	58	1

PUNT RETURNS

PUNT RETURNS	No.	FC	Yds.	Avg.	LG	TD
Mike Nelms	32	0	252	7.9	28	0
Nick Giaquinto	5	2	34	6.8	12	0
Greg Williams	1	0	9	9.0	9	0
REDSKINS TOTAL	38	2	295	7.8	28	0
Opp. Total	30	2	106	3.5	11	0

KICKOFF RETURNS

KICKOFF RETURNS	No.	Yds.	Avg.	LG	TD
Mike Nelms	23	557	24.2	58	0
Nick Giaquinto	1	21	21.0	21	0
Alvin Garrett	2	35	17.5	18	0
Otis Wonsley	1	14	14.0	14	0
Clarence Harmon	1	13	13.0	13	0
Stuart Anderson	1	7	7.0	7	0
Greg Williams	1	2	2.0	2	0
REDSKINS TOTAL	30	649	21.6	58	0
Opp. Total	41	728	17.8	33	0

Moseley (30,48,26) (35, 21, 19) (39, 29) (45, 43) (38) (32, 30, 20, 24) (20, 31, 42) (36, 45) (40)

WASHINGTON REDSKINS PLAYOFF STATISTICS

RESULTS AND ATTENDANCE (Actual)
1982 PLAYOFF RESULTS

January 8	31	Detroit Lions	7	55,045
January 15	21	Minnesota Vikings	7	54,593
January 22	31	Dallas Cowboys	17	55,045

TEAM STATISTICS

	Redskins	Opponent
TOTAL FIRST DOWNS	59	56
Rushing	33	11
Passing	24	42
Penalty	2	3
3rd Down: Made/Att.	19-40 (47.5%)	20-42 (47.6%)
4th Down: Made/Att.	2-3	0-4
TOTAL NET YARDS	1041	1021
Avg. Per Game	347.0	340.3
Total Plays	189	187
Avg. Per Play	5.5	5.5
NET YARDS RUSHING	516	239
Avg. Per Game	172.0	79.7
Total Rushes	120	60
NET YARDS PASSING	525	782
Avg. Per Game	175.0	260.7
Tackled/Yards Lost	7-48	6-43
Gross Yards	573	825
Attempts/Completions	62-43	121-63
Pct. of Completions	69.4	52.1
Had Intercepted	1	4
PUNTS/AVERAGE	11-35.1	10-36.5
NET PUNTING AVG.	31.2	28.2
PENALTIES/YARDS	10/70	13/83
FUMBLES/BALL LOST	1-0	6-4
TOUCHDOWNS	11	4
Rushing	3	1
Passing	6	3
Returns	2	0

SCORE BY PERIODS

	1	2	3	4	OT	Total
REDSKINS TOTAL	31	28	14	10		83
Opp. Total	3	7	21	0		31

SCORING

	TDR	TDP	TDRt	PAT	FG	S	TP
Alvin Garrett		4					24
John Riggins	3						18
Mark Moseley				11-11	2-6		17
Jeris White			1				6
Charlie Brown		1					6
Darryl Grant			1				6
Don Warren		1					6
REDSKIN TOTAL	3	6	2	11-11	2-6		83
Opp. Total	1	3	0	4-4	1-2		31

FIELD GOALS

	1-19	20-29	30-39	40-49	50+	Total
Mark Moseley	0-0	2-3	0-1	0-2		2-6
REDSKINS TOTAL	0-0	2-3	0-1	0-2		2-6
Opp. Total	0-0	1-1	0-1	0-1		1-3

PASSING

	Att.	Comp.	Yards	Pct.	Avg./Att.	TD	Pct. TD	Int.	Pct. Int.	LG	Lost/Att.	Rating
Joe Theismann	62	43	573	69.4	9.24	6	9.7	1	1.6	46	7/48	124.1
REDSKINS TOTAL	62	43	573	69.4	9.24	6	9.7	1	1.6	46	7/48	124.1
Opp. Total	121	63	825	52.1	6.82	3	2.5	4	3.3	48	6/43	68.5

RUSHING

	No.	Yds.	Avg.	LG	TD
John Riggins	98	444	4.5	29	3
Wilbur Jackson	8	27	3.4	7	0
Joe Washington	4	22	5.5	11	0
Rick Walker	2	14	7.0	9	0
Joe Theismann	6	7	1.2	9	0
Alvin Garrett	2	2	1.0	4	0
REDSKINS TOTAL	120	516	4.3	29	3
Opp. Total	60	239	4.0	18	1

RECEIVING

	No.	Yds.	Avg.	LG	TD
Alvin Garrett	13	231	17.8	46	4
Charlie Brown	11	182	16.5	45	1
Rick Walker	7	40	5.7	9	0
Don Warren	6	44	7.3	15	1
Joe Washington	3	33	11.0	13	0
Nick Giaquinto	2	39	19.5	29	0
Clarence Harmon	1	4	4.0	4	0
REDSKINS TOTAL	43	573	13.3	46	6
Opp. Total	63	825	13.1	48	3

INTERCEPTIONS

	No.	Yds.	Avg.	LG	TD
Jeris White	2	77	38.5	77t	1
Darryl Grant	1	10	10.0	10	1
Mel Kaufman	1	2	2.0	2	0
REDSKINS TOTAL	4	89	22.3	77	2
Opp. Total	1	0	0.0	0	0

PUNTING

	No.	Yds.	Avg.	TB	In 20	LG	Blk.
Jeff Hayes	11	386	35.1	1	2	48	0
REDSKINS TOTAL	11	386	35.1	1	2	48	0
Opp. Total	10	365	36.5	0	0	61	0

PUNT RETURNS

	No.	FC	Yds.	Avg.	LG	TD
Mike Nelms	6	0	83	13.8	39	0
REDSKINS TOTAL	6	0	83	13.8	39	0
Opp. Total	5	1	23	4.6	8	0

KICKOFF RETURNS

	No.	Yds.	Avg.	LG	TD
Mike Nelms	7	187	26.7	76	0
Wilbur Jackson	1	18	18.0	18	0
REDSKINS TOTAL	8	205	25.6	76	0
Opp. Total	14	272	19.4	33	0

Moseley (26, 42 wide right)
(47 wide left, 39 wide right)
(27 left, 29)

191

PLAYOFF DEFENSIVE STATS

	Name	Pos	Tack	Ass't	Totals
1.	Mark Murphy	FS	19	13	32
2.	Neal Olkewicz	LB	15	8	23
3.	Vernon Dean	CB	17	5	22
4.	Jeris White	DB	15	3	18
5.	Tony Peters	SS	12	4	16
6.	Dave Butz	DT	10	4	14
7.	Rich Milot	LB	8	6	14
8.	Mel Kaufman	LB	6	6	12
9.	Dexter Manley	DE	8	0	8
10.	Monte Coleman	LB	6	1	7
11.	Mat Mendenhall	DE	3	4	7
12.	Darryl Grant	DT	4	3	7
13.	Tony McGee	DE	2	1	3
14.	Curtis Jordan	SS	1	2	3
15.	Pat Ogrin	DT	1	1	2
16.	Todd Liebenstein	DE	1	0	1
17.	Larry Kubin	LB	0	1	1
18.	Joe Lavender	CB	1	0	1

Sacks

Dexter Manley	2
Monte Coleman	1
Mark Murphy	1
Vernon Dean	1
Tony McGee	1
	6

Forced Fumbles

Dave Butz	2
Vernon Dean	1
Tony Peters	1
	4

Recovered Fumbles

Dexter Manley	1
Darryl Grant	1
Rich Milot	1
Monte Coleman	1
	4

FINAL REGULAR SEASON STATS

	Name	Pos	Tack	Ass't	Totals
1.	Mark Murphy	FS	55	45	100
2.	Neal Olkewicz	LB	55	33	88
3.	Rich Milot	LB	41	32	73
4.	Dave Butz	DT	37	18	55
5.	Tony Peters	SS	28	23	51
6.	Mel Kaufman	LB	25	24	49
7.	Dexter Manley	DE	32	16	48
8.	Vernon Dean	CB	34	13	47
9.	Jeris White	DB	22	19	41
10.	Darryl Grant	DT	24	13	37
11.	Mat Mendenhall	DE	17	17	34
12.	Monte Coleman	LB	22	5	27
13.	Perry Brooks	DT	17	4	21
14.	Larry Kubin	LB	9	5	14
15.	Joe Lavender	CB	10	0	10
16.	Tony McGee	DE	7	2	9
17.	Todd Liebenstein	DE	3	2	5
18.	Curtis Jordan	FS	1	3	4
19.	LeCharls McDaniel	CB	3	0	3
20.	Quentin Lowry	LB	0	2	2
21.	Peter Cronan	LB	1	0	1

Sacks

Dexter Manley	6½
Tony McGee	6½
Dave Butz	4½
Darryl Grant	3
Rich Milot	3
Neal Olkewicz	2½
Mel Kaufman	2
Perry Brooks	1
Todd Liebenstein	1
Mark Murphy	1
Larry Kubin	½
Mat Mendenhall	½
	32

Forced Fumbles

Rich Milot	4
Neal Olkewicz	1
Vernon Dean	1
Perry Brooks	1
Dexter Manley	1
Mark Murphy	1
Dave Butz	1
	10

Recovered Fumbles

Neal Olkewicz	3
Dexter Manley	3
Joe Lavender	1
Perry Brooks	1
Tony Peters	1
Mel Kaufman	1
Larry Kubin	1
Otis Wonsley	1
Dave Butz	1
	11